Late Have I Loved You

An Interpretation of

SAINT AUGUSTINE
*On Human
And Divine Relationships*

Late Have I
Loved You

James A. Mohler S.J.

Published in the United States by New City Press
206 Skillman Avenue, Brooklyn, New York 11211
©1991 New City Press, New York

Cover design by Nick Cianfarani

Library of Congress Cataloging-in-Publication Data:

Mohler, James A.
    Late have I loved you : an interpretation of Saint Augustine on
  human and divine relationships / James A. Mohler.
      p.   cm.
    Includes bibliographical references and index.
    ISBN 0-911782-86-9 : $8.95
      1. Augustine, Saint, Bishop of Hippo.   2. Theology, Doctrinal—
  History—Early church, ca. 30-600.   I. Title.
  BR65.A9M56   1991
  230'.14—dc20   90-28643

Printed in the United States of America

TABLE OF CONTENTS

PROLOGUE

Augustine rightly has been called the greatest of the Western Fathers, and, in a sense, the founder of Western Christian theology. His broad background in education and rhetoric both as a student and teacher and his deep interest in philosophy gave him a good foundation for his future career as pastor, bishop and defender of the faith.

Augustine's free life as a student and teacher before his conversion he relates in his *Confessions,* a classic which has inspired generations going through the same struggles.

Augustine's pastoral concern may be seen in all his works from his *Confessions* to his treatises against heretics and his many sermons and letters. Some have called him the patron of mediocre Christians, for he recognized his own weaknesses and so was compassionate and patient with the faults of others. Moreover, he chastised the rigidity of some heresies that were short on forgiveness.

These essays discuss some of Augustine's views on human and divine relationships, from the problem of suffering, faith and love, matrimony and religious life to education and social justice.

It is our small hope that we mediocre Christians of the modern world may gain some insights into Augustine's interior path. "I was outside, you were inside."

I.
INTRODUCTION

Life

Augustine was born in Thagaste in the province of Numidia Proconsularis in the year 354. His family was of moderate means; his pagan father Patricius was a busy local Roman official, while his saintly mother Monica inspired the conversion of both her husband and son. Though educated in the Christian catechumenate, Augustine's baptism was delayed until adulthood according to the custom of the time.

As Augustine grew into teenage, he was attracted to the pleasures of the flesh, especially when he went to the pagan city of Carthage for studies in 370. There he took up with a slave girl concubine in an unequal marriage, not unusual among students of the time. She bore him a son Adeodatus. Augustine would remain faithful to her for fifteen years until he sent her away shortly before his baptism. He never mentions her by name.

In his rhetorical studies Augustine became enamored of the great Roman orator Cicero and his love of wisdom and henceforward Augustine was drawn more to philosophy than to rhetoric.

At the time Persian Manicheanism, a combination of Zoroastrianism and Christianity, was popular in Africa. Augustine was attracted to its pseudointellectualism, its penchant to delve into nature's secrets and its search for an answer to the problem of evil in an opposition between dark and light. Also he felt that their external cause of evil freed him from any culpability for his own sins.[1]

Augustine pursued his career as a rhetor in Thagaste and Carthage. Some of his pupils would become his lifelong companions.

Like most young people, Augustine was searching for answers. Though at first he thought the Manicheans had the right solutions, he

---

1. E. Portalié, *A Guide to the Thought of Saint Augustine* (Chicago: Regnery, 1960), 9.

was soon disillusioned by their ignorance, immorality and negative view of life.

In 383 Augustine moved to Rome to start a rhetorical school. Then on to a professorship in Milan. He was attracted to the philosophy of the Academics and the Neoplatonists. In the latter he found many answers to his questions about God, truth, goodness, beauty, etc. With his friends he wanted to found a philosophical school like those of classical times. Also he was inspired by his readings of sacred scriptures and by the holiness and wisdom of bishop Ambrose. These along with his mother's incessant prayers encouraged his conversion and baptism by Ambrose in 387.

For a while during 386-87 Augustine and his friends were happy philosophers at Cassiciacum, the country estate of a friend, delving into the meaning of truth, happiness, providence, evil, God and the soul. Augustine tried to parallel the teachings of Plato with those of his religion, combining philosophy and faith.[1] He also developed his prayer life at Cassiciacum.

After his mother's death, Augustine returned to Thagaste in 388. There he founded a small monastery and continued his philosophical discussions and writings.

Chosen a priest by the people of Hippo in 391, he was noted for his preaching, pastoral care and opposition to heretics. He was consecrated coadjutor bishop of Hippo in 396. There he continued his monastic way with his clergy living in the episcopal residence. Many of his colleagues would become leaders in the African Church. Augustine himself was a model of religious life in his poverty, austerity and charity.

His pastoral concern for his flock is shown especially in his sermons and letters. Moderation and sympathy with the weakness of human nature were his guides.

Correcting Errors

It was in the spirit of pastoral worry that Augustine attacked various errors that were pervading the church, especially Manicheanism, Donatism and Arianism. Having been a Manichean proselyte, Augustine was anxious to help his former companions to see the true light as he did, engaging them in oral and written debate.

Like the Novatians, the Donatists wanted to restrict church mem-

---

1. *Ibid.*, 117.

bership to the saints and some became quite militant in defense of their beliefs.

But Augustine did not retaliate. Rather, because of his own early mistakes, he was patient with those who unwittingly had joined questionable sects, preferring tolerance to vindictiveness. He inspired the African councils to show a conciliatory friendliness toward the Donatists. For example, allowing the converted Donatist clergy to keep their orders in the Catholic Church.[1] However, when some Donatists remained militant against the Catholics, the bishops appealed to Emperor Honorius. Yet Augustine continued to encourage the conversion of heretical bishops and their flocks, stressing dialogue over severe penalties.

In the Conference at Carthage in 411 Augustine again showed his sympathy with sinners, noting that the church was created to heal and not to spurn them.

The Celtic monk Pelagius (Morgan) went in another direction, teaching the necessary part of human strength on the road to salvation. The Carthage synod (411) condemned the doctrines of Pelagius and his disciple Celestius. Also Augustine answered Pelagius in his work *On Nature and Grace* (415), teaching the importance of divine grace for spiritual health. Though some Eastern bishops defended Pelagius, the pope and African bishops (418) held firm, stressing the dogma of original sin and the necessity of grace.

When some Italian bishops took up Pelagius' cause, Augustine engaged bishop Julian in a long debate. But some felt that Augustine had gone too far in his condemnation of Pelagius and Julian. For if everything depends on God's grace, of what use is our free will? Some Gaulicans hoped to find a compromise between Pelagius and Augustine, nature and grace, so that grace would only be given to those who merit it. For one must ask before he can receive. However, Augustine countered that even the beginnings of desires for eternal life demand God's help so that God entirely controls our predestination. John Cassian responded in his thirteenth conference with the desert Fathers (426). Then Prosper of Aquitaine defended Augustine, with each side accusing the other of exaggerations.[2]

Marrou does not like the term Semipelagian, since it was a natural reaction to exaggerated Augustinianism and had strong roots in the teachings of the Greek Fathers.[3] The Gaulic dispute continued until the Council of Orange (529) when Semipelagianism was condemned.

---

1. *Ibid.*, 26.
2. H. Marrou, *Saint Augustine and His Influence through the Ages* (New York: Harper and Brothers), 149.
3. *Ibid.*, 150.

The result of the dialogue was the evolution of a moderate Augustinianism.

Augustine's last battle was against the popular Arian heresy, brought into Italy and Africa by the Goths and Vandals. The Goths were sent into Africa by the Empress Placidia to fight against the recalcitrant Count Boniface, who requested aid from the Vandals. Augustine tried in vain to reconcile Boniface and Placidia. But when Boniface sought refuge in Hippo, there ensued an eighteen-month siege.

Augustine died in 430 at the age of seventy-six after a long life of study, preaching, writing and pastoral care.

Synthesis

Marrou comments, "We have to wait for the bishop of Hippo before we find a Western theology truly complete which has become autonomous and fully formed."[1] Augustine is the first and last of the great Latin Fathers. Though the Germanic invasions slowed Western thought and culture, Augustine's influence was carried on by men like Fulgentius of Ruspa, Isidore of Seville, Caesarius of Arles and Gregory the Great.[2]

Augustine's authority was felt not only in the evolution of dogma, but also in the growth of Western monasticism. Marrou sees the Western monastic stream flowing from two sources: Egypt and the desert Fathers, and Africa and Augustine.[3]

As Aquinas was to be the great synthesizer of thirteenth century thought, so Augustine in the fifth century. Portalié remarks, "Augustine collects and condenses in his writings the intellectual treasures of the old world and transmits them to the new."[4] Just what was needed — someone to syncretize the best of ancient thought, Christian and pagan, a man schooled in the classics (Latin and Christian). Augustine passed on his wisdom to the rude immigrants, grafting the prized vine of ancient culture onto the strong wild roots of the Barbarian peoples.

Portalié notes three worlds that helped shape Augustine's thought: the Latin world of classical rhetoric; glimpses of Eastern wisdom in

---

1. *Ibid.*, 152-53.
2. *Ibid.*, 154-55.
3. *Ibid.*, 155.
4. E. Portalié, *A Guide to the Thought of Saint Augustine,* 84.

the doctrine of Mani; the Greek ideas in the writings of the Neoplatonists.[1]

Augustine helped crystalize Christian thought up to his day. However, he is not a summist. Rather he digests the best of Christian and classical traditions, making them his own. As Euken comments, "From primitive Christianity and Neoplatonism he worked out a new synthesis in which the Christian element, with his own originality, is predominant."[2]

Augustine was a major mover in the development of Christian dogma, a second Paul. "Thus the words of the gospel increase, rendered fruitful by providential geniuses, of whom Augustine seems to be the greatest of all,"[3] justifying, clarifying and explaining Christian revelation for the people of his time.

Augustine had a great yearning for the truth which led him to investigate everything from evil to love, creation, the Trinity, church, religious life, marriage, etc., guarding his flock from the many errors of those volatile times. No doubt his training as a rhetor helped him to translate deep mysteries into readable treatises.

He made special contributions in the evolution of the dogmas of original sin, atonement, grace and predestination. His arguments against the Donatists helped develop Augustine's ecclesiology, showing the church as the salvific body of Christ. Moreover, his reactions to the Manicheans merited him the titles of "Doctor of the Good" and "Doctor of Charity."[4]

With Augustine the center of dogmatic and theological development shifted from the East to the West.[5] Boniface remarks, "The practical, realistic spirit of the Latin race supplants the speculative and idealistic spirit of the East and Greece."[6]

Augustine has been called the first modern man, the first psychologist, etc. His thought is God-centered, stressing the mutual love of God and the human soul. God descended so that we can ascend.

Now let us examine in detail some of Augustine's wisdom, beginning with the problem of evil.

---

1. *Ibid.*, 85.
2. Euken quoted by Portalié, *A Guide to the Thought of Saint Augustine*, 85.
3. *Ibid.*, 86.
4. *Ibid.*, 87.
5. *Ibid.*
6. *Ibid.*

II.
BETTER TO BRING GOOD OUT OF EVIL

(Enchiridion, 27)

The Problem of Evil

The problem of evil has plagued humans since the beginning. How can a good God allow sickness, death, crime, etc., in his universe? Solutions varied from creation stories about tricksters or punishments vented on disobedient men and women by the vengeful gods. However, in none of the myths is evil a part of God's original plan, but rather an aberration from it.

Zoroastrians, Gnostics and Manicheans taught a dualist or semi-dualist explanation. The Zoroastrians influenced the Judaeo/Christian belief in the battle between the forces of light and the forces of dark, which became personified in the struggle between Christ and Satan.

For some Greek philosophers like Plato matter seems to be the source of evil so that our freedom is found in our flight upwards from the material to the spiritual. For Aristotle the prime mover, perfect and immutable, is the sole source of good, order and unity in the universe, while indeterminate matter brings about evil. Plotinus, who influenced Augustine, said that providence, the perfect world soul influenced the world so that events that appear to be evil can be useful for world order. The physical world emanates from the one, good deity. And human individuality which unites being and non-being can be healed by divine union, reversing the emanation line.

Shortly after his conversion and baptism (386-87), Augustine began his attack on Manichean dualism, while starting to formulate his own solution to the problem of evil and suffering in the world. The loving divine providence had carried Augustine through his gloomy moments at his Cassiciacum retreat when his brilliant academic career was collapsing around him. So it is fitting that his earliest dialogues concern providence and evil.

Order and Disorder

Augustine attempts to answer the dilemma of the good God and evil in the world in his discussion of world order.[1] He firmly believed in the compatibility of evil with the divine plan, an idea he was to develop further when speaking of free choice and other answers to the Manicheans.

At first glance, there seems to be a contradiction between the existence of evil and suffering in the world and a loving divine providence. Augustine rightly observes that we tend to blow up tiny fragments of the universe way out of proportion. For example, if we look closely at one small piece of tile in a large and beautiful mosaic on the floor of Augustine's basilica at Hippo, it seems to be shapeless and even ugly all by itself. However, when we step back to admire the whole picture in a proper perspective we see that the tessera is just a tiny dot in the overall plan of the artist. And it fits in perfectly. So we are liable to think that our whole world is disarranged, when some small part of it displeases us.

We can see the master design of the universe by withdrawing ourselves from ephemeral sense objects and going within ourselves. This is what Augustine tried to do during his Cassiciacum retreat. For the more our soul tries to grasp material things, the more it suffers want. "The soul, spreading out from itself, is battered by a kind of immensity and worn out in the quality of a beggar, because its nature forces it to seek everywhere that which is one, and the multitude does not permit it to find unity" (1, 2).

Though God loves order, he does not love the evil that is a part of that order. Human suffering and disorder are part of God's plan. Even prostitutes and hangmen have their place. Likewise in the human body "the ugly members, by keeping their place, have provided a better position for the comely ones" (2, 4).

Since evil is against nature, God, who is the cause of nature, cannot at the same time be the cause of evil, Augustine explains to the Manicheans.[2]

There are two types of good. The first is good in itself and this is God. The second is good by participation. These are creatures which are liable to be hurt by their falling away.

Complex creatures imitate divine unity by the agreement of their parts and so they exist. On the other hand, disorder, perversion and corruption lead to non-existence. So anything that is corrupted is on

---

1. *Order*, sometimes called *The Problem of Evil* (386) (F). References that follow a citation refer to that citation unless otherwise noted.
2. *Morals of the Manicheans* (388), chap. 2 (N).

the way to non-existence. Though God does not allow corruption to spread all the way to annihilation, he permits things to fall back until they recover. Thus sinners suffer according to the divine judgment (7).

Whatever falls away from being is not of God. "Yet it is ordered by divine providence in agreement with the whole system." Though evil is a disagreement hostile to a substance, it might not be harmful to another substance. For example, although a scorpion's poison is good for itself, it is bad for us. Also the four elements can help or harm.

Free Choice

Augustine believes that evil in the world is due to our errant free will, rather than an evil material nature as the Manicheans taught.[1] Though God is not the author of the bad things that we do, he is the author of the evil that we suffer to correct us.

But what is doing evil? For example, is adultery bad because it is forbidden, or is it forbidden because it is bad? Evil does not come from an outside force, but rather from within. Immorality for Augustine, echoing Plato, is a turning away from good, God, to creatures who are but reflections of divine goodness and beauty. Moreover, this error is against the eternal law. For the temporal law does not forbid our attachment to creatures, but rather that we should not injure others in our pell-mell pursuit of them. "There would be no punishment inflicted on people either by injury done them or by legal sentence, if they did not love the things that can be taken from them against their wills" (1, 15). We tend to make ourselves slaves of money and sex instead of having them serve us.

If we use our goods rightly, we will not become attached to them, making them parts of our soul, "lest when they begin to be taken from us, we suffer torture and decay." This is an important cornerstone of Augustine's theology of suffering. For our suffering is not caused by some evil object, but rather by our corrupt ego's attachment to a good creature.

For example, gold does not make us covetous; or wine make us drunks; or shapely legs and breasts turn us into lusters. All of these things God created good. But we can, by our free wills, use them in an evil manner. Why do we partake of these beautiful creatures wrongly? Augustine says that it is our corrupted sense of free choice. For God would not punish or reward us unless we act freely (2, 1).

---

1. *Free Will* (388-) 1, 1 (N).

All things, inferior and superior, contribute to the universe. And there is a parallel in the role of souls as well. "The fact that there are souls which ought to be miserable because they willed to be sinful, contributes to the perfection of the universe." And again. "Neither the sins nor the misery are necessary to the perfection of the universe, but souls as such are necessary which have the power to sin if they so will and become miserable if they sin."

Augustine seems to go along with the common belief that suffering is a punishment for sin. But whereas the voluntary state of sin is dishonorable, the penal state of suffering for sin is good. "Indeed, it compels the dishonorable state to become harmonized with the honor of the universe so that the penalty of sin corrects the dishonor of sin." For one who disobeys God's law must pay his debt. "If the soul does not pay its debt by doing what it ought, it will pay it by suffering what it ought to suffer." Moreover, no interval can come between fault and suffering, lest the beauty of the universe be defiled by sin. So "he who does not do what he ought immediately suffers what he ought . . . For such is the happiness of doing justly that no one can part from it without immediately finding misery" (3, 15).

For every sinful soul there were two penal conditions: ignorance and difficulty. "From ignorance springs disgraceful error and from difficulty painful effort . . . To prove falsehood instead of truth so as to err in spite of himself, and not to be able to refrain from the works of lust because of the pain involved in breaking away from the fleshly bonds" (3, 18). These were not part of the original creation package, but the penalty of condemned mankind. Some people blame Adam and Eve for their sufferings, but they forget about their personal sins. Moreover, they should remember that Adam is Everyman and Eve is Everywoman.

But what about infants who suffer and die before they reach the age of sin? God never creates anything in vain. "Perhaps God is doing some good in correcting parents when their beloved children suffer pain and even death" (3, 23). "By the torments of their children, parents have their hard hearts softened, their faith exercised and their tenderness proved." Augustine had sadly buried his only son.

Even after his conversion, Augustine still feels defiled by vain things.[1] And he wonders whether God can be a spatial being. For though he is all good, true, incorruptible, immutable and superior to the corruptible and changeable, it seems that he is also infinitely spatial and so filling the whole of heaven and earth.

Augustine rejects the Manichean view, namely, that "your sub-stance is subject to evil, rather than that their own substance committed

---

1. *Confessions* (397-401) 7, 1-5. 12. 13. 16.

evil" (7, 3). While our free will causes evil, God's just judgment causes our own suffering evil.

But Augustine still does not understand it. If the good God made him good, why does he will evil? Even the devil was created by the good divinity.

God is absolute good. "What he wills for himself is good, and he himself is that good." But if God is good and has created all things good, how does evil creep into the picture? What is its root and seed? Or does evil even exist? And "why do we fear what does not exist?" Even the fear of evil is evil. Is the evil matter of the Manicheans the cause of evil in the world? Did the Creator leave some evil in creation, and if so, is it eternal?

Augustine comments, "It is clear to me that suffering beings are nonetheless good" (7, 12). However, if they are supremely good, they are incorruptible. For otherwise they would be damaged and so not supremely good.

What is corrupted is deprived of a good. However, if it is deprived of all good, it is annihilated. "As long as things exist, they are good." Moreover, evil cannot be a substance, for otherwise it would be good. All things are good and all things taken together are very good.

To God all things are good and there is order in the universe (7, 13). But to us "among the parts of the universe some things are thought to be evil because they do not agree with other parts." However, they are in synch with other elements and so are good. Though they may seem to us to be out of harmony, they fit well into the overall plan of God.

We should never say that certain things should not exist. Maybe they seem to be bad when they are seen individually. But we should still thank God for them. The earth, dragons, deeps, fire, hail, snow, ice, storm, winds, mountains, hills, trees, beasts, snakes, birds, kings, people, old and young, all praise Yahweh's name. Augustine begins to see the whole divine plan which is superior to its individual parts.

What is iniquity? It is not a substance, but rather a certain perversity of will twisted away from God toward creatures (7, 16).

Christian Combat [1]

Writing on the Christian's lifelong battle for good and against evil, Bishop Augustine guides the faithful of Hippo in their struggle against

---

1. *The Christian Combat* (397) 7, 8 (F).

Satan, while exposing certain Manichean errors. Though life is full of pains, we should be happy and hopeful of an eternal reward.

> Now should we be unsettled because during this life the just endure many grave and bitter hardships by reason of the body they carry about? If in this life, where so much affliction is found, the good and just cannot only endure patiently when suffering such trials, but can glory in the love of God, what are we to think of the life promised to us, wherein we should experience no bodily discomfort? (7, 8)

When temporal goods are taken away, the deprived suffer and those who confiscate them are gleeful. But their joy is short. Like that of a hungry fish who joyfully snaps up a tasty worm in which a sharp hook is imbedded. However, the wicked can cause no suffering in the good, since they cannot deprive them of what they love. No one can steal from them the object of their love and the source of their happiness. "In fact, bodily suffering makes wicked souls miserable, but borne with fortitude, it purifies souls that are good." Even wicked people and bad angels can be unwitting instruments of our purification, bringing us joy in our pains, as the vicious Roman carnifices pounded the sharp nails into the tender flesh of the smiling martyrs who had eyes only for eternal life.

Augustine teaches the value of suffering rightly undergone and the lack of worth of earthly pleasures. "Do not be afraid of insults, crosses and death, for if these were harmful to man, the human nature assumed by the Son of God would not have suffered them" (9, 10). On the other hand, Jesus avoided carnal pleasures and wealth as ways to happiness.

Jesus is the Proto-Martyr, the paradigm of Christian suffering. Like a healing shaman, he leads his followers through his pains and his victory over death.

> O Medicine, making provision for all, deflating what is distended, renewing what is wasting away, cutting away what is superfluous, preserving what is necessary, restoring what has been lost, curing what is corrupted . . . Who can believe what happiness is to be found in those things which the Son of God has taught us to despise? What tribulation can overcome him who believes that in the Son of God human nature was preserved intact amid violent persecution? (11, 12)

Evil, the Corruption of a Good Nature [1]

Every nature is created good by God. For example, when the pollution is filtered out of water, the remaining fluid is clear and clean. So nature is purer when evil is removed, but is annihilated when its good is taken away. And in natural phenomena such as high winds, "the disagreeable things are additions to nature." So when these bad aspects are eliminated, the natures are better. However, if we take away the good, no natures remain (33).

Evil is basically corruption. Thus the corruption of the mind is ignorance, while the decay of health is sickness; the weakening of strength is exhaustion; rest is worn out by toil; beauty by ugliness; straightness by the crooked. "Corruption does harm only in displacing the natural condition. So corruption is not nature, but rather it is against nature." Therefore, nature itself is not evil (35).

Corruption tends toward non-existence. For example, while the human body gradually builds itself up as an infant, youth, etc., it grows into more and more existence. But then as it becomes enfeebled, weak and ugly in old age, it heads downhill toward non-existence. "In proportion as anything is corrupted, in that proportion it approaches decease or non-existence" (40).

Why does God allow corruption to take away from the good natures which he has created? Corruption can harm nothing unless God permits it.

As our words disappear in silence even while we are speaking, so temporal creatures come and go in birth and death.

When distress comes to us through their peculiar beauty by the loss of beloved temporal things passing away, we both pay the penalty of our sins and are exhorted to set our affection on eternal things. (41)

Since God is the highest good, he is also unchangeable.[2] However, all other good things are made by him out of nothing and so are changeable.

Since all things in nature are good in their measure, form and order, evil is a corruption of measure, form and order. Moreover, when nature is corrupted, "so far as it is nature, it is good; but insofar as it is corrupted, it is evil" (4).

Though God is the highest good, every created nature that is corruptible is also some good. And corruption cannot injure it except

---

1. *Answer to the Letter of Mani Known as "The Foundation"* (397), 33 (N).
2. *The Nature of the Good* (405), 1 (N).

by diminishing its good (6). Corruption in humans can be voluntary in our sins or involuntary through our punishment for sin (7).

Pain exists only in good natures (20). "When a being is compelled to something better, the pain is useful, but when to something worse it is useless." Since for Augustine pain and suffering are privations of the good, they can only be experienced in a good nature. "For the very fact of resistance in any being, leading to pain, involves a refusal to be what it was, because it was something good" (21).

The power to be harmful to another comes from God (32). "It is not unrighteous that by the wicked, receiving the power of being hurtful, both the patience of the good should be proved and the iniquity of the evil punished." For example, God gave Satan permission to test Job.

Sin is not so much the striving after an evil nature, as it is the desertion of a better one. Thus in the Garden of Eden Adam and Eve left the better (God) for the forbidden fruit of the Tree of Knowledge. The tree was not evil, but it is better to obey God (36).

An Evil Person Is an Evil Good

In his handbook of the Christian faith[1] Augustine writes of Adam and original sin against the Pelagians who had misused his earlier work on *Free Will*.

The supremely good Creator made all things good, but not supremely good. "Taken as a whole, however, they are very good, because their ensemble constitutes the universe in all its wonderful order and beauty" (10). Even the evil has its role as the absence of good.

> For when it is regulated and put in its own place, it only enhances our admiration of the good more when we compare it with the evil. (11)

Furthermore, the almighty good God "would never permit the existence of anything evil among his works, if he were not so omnipotent and good that he can bring good even out of evil." Evil disease is the absence of good health. So when we are cured, our disease disappears and our flesh is restored because our sickness is not a good substance, but rather an accident or a privation of wellness.

Since creation was not made perfectly good, it is liable to corruption, diminution and increase. But "so long as a being is in the process of

---

1. *Enchiridion* (421) 10.

corruption, there is in it some good of which it is being corrupted." For if it were wholly corrupted, it would cease to exist.

An evil person is an evil good, for there can be no evil where there is no good. The good, wholly without evil, is perfect good, while the good which contains evil is an imperfect good (13). "Nothing can be evil except something which is good." However, good can exist without evil. Insofar as we are an angel or a human being we are good and insofar as we are wicked, we are evil (14).

Evil and suffering are privations of good. For example, death, Adam's punishment, is a denial of life. We all inherit original sin and are drawn by it,

> through diverse errors and sufferings into the last end and endless punishment which they suffer in common with the fallen angels, their corrupters and masters, and the partakers of their doom. (27)

Yet despite our sinful inheritance, God still allows us to propagate and gives us food, sustenance and protection. "For he judged it better to bring good out of evil, than not to permit any evil to exist."

God permits evil according to his just judgment. "The fact that evil as well as good exists is a good. For otherwise God would not permit it" (96). Furthermore, God's will is sometimes fulfilled by the evil wills of certain people. "God accomplishes some of his purposes — all good — through the evil desires of wicked people" (101). For example, those who were responsible for the death of Christ. God's will is never defeated and never evil, writes Augustine. "Even when the will of God inflicts evil, it is just" and so not evil.

Augustine popularized the doctrine of original sin, based on the Pauline and rabbinical *yetzer ha-ra* (evil influence). This tendency to sin is passed down the line of the human race from its sinful progenitors, Adam and Eve. Augustine taught original sin as a counterbalance to the Pelagians who overstressed our natural human abilities. Moreover, he believed that the newborn baby not only inherits the sin of Adam and Eve, but also the faults of.his parents. And all the more reason for infant baptism. However, there is hope. For as through one person came sin, suffering and death, so through one person, the second Adam, Jesus Christ, we receive grace, salvation and life.

Two Cities

Augustine further discusses the problem of good and evil in his tale of the two cities of God and mankind.[1] "It is the nature of a good God to create good things." Scripture tells us that "God saw all that he had made was very good" (Gn 1:51). Augustine comments: "There was no other reason for creating the world except that good creatures might be made by a good God." Moreover, if no one had sinned, "this beautiful world would have been filled with created natures that are good."

However, even the sinfulness of a will, refusing to preserve the order of its nature can lessen the beauty of God's total order, "designed, as it is, according to the laws of justice." As a painting is not harmed by dark coloring, "so the beauty of the universe of creatures (if one has the insight to discern it) is not marred by sins, even though sin itself is an ugly blotch."

Three questions can be asked about a creature: Who made it? How? And why? Three answers: God. By his Word. And because it is good. Perhaps there is a Trinitarian reflection here.

Our sins are not bad for God. But rather they harm ourselves. Sin is evil because what is good in our nature is wounded. Nevertheless, it is not our nature, but the wound in our nature that is opposed to God, as evil is opposed to good (12, 3).

Since God is supremely good, any lack of goodness is against him. But even then "the harm done bears witness to the goodness of the natures which suffer." For unless they were good, they would not suffer from any lack of goods. For example, the loss of integrity, beauty, health, virtue, or any other good lost or lessened by sin or sickness. "No nature can be damaged by a defect unless that nature itself is good."

Though good things without defects can sometimes be found, there are no absolutely bad things. Moreover, corruptible goods are evil only insofar as they are defective and good insofar as they are natural. Furthermore, when our sinful nature is punished, it becomes better because of God's good justice.

But what about defects and suffering found in animals? Certainly they have not sinned.

It was the will of the Creator that they received that measure of being whereby their comings and goings and fleeting existences should contribute to that special, if lowly, loveliness of our

---

1. *City of God* (413-26), 11, 23 (F). Next few quotes are from here.

earthly seasons, which chimes with the harmony of the universe. (12, 4)

The law of transitory things, involving birth and death, and the strong over the weak contributes to the beauty of world order. Sometimes we do not see this because we are too absorbed in ourselves. So "we fail to notice the beauty of the whole pattern in which the particular parts, which seem ugly to us, blend in so harmonious and beautiful a way." If we cannot understand the wisdom of God's providence, we should believe anyway, rather than criticize the master plan of creation.

Defects in earthly things reveal their good natures, created by God. Good elements, such as fire, can either harm or help us. All natures are good, because they exist, having their own being, beauty and peace, if they remain in their proper place.

Lower creatures promote the common good by their changes, following the design of divine providence.

The dissolution which brings mutable and mortal things to their death is not so much a process of annihilation, as a progress toward something they were intended to become. (12, 5)

God should not be blamed for defects that offend us. Rather we should praise him for the perfection of nature.

So much for corruption in lower forms, but what causes moral evil in humans? "An evil will is the efficient cause of a bad action. But there is no efficient cause of an evil will." Rather there is a deficient cause. "The fault of an evil will begins when one falls from the Supreme Being to some being which is less than absolute" (12, 7).

God cannot be blamed for the evil in the world, since he can only cause good. Rather it is our corrupt will that brings about sin. Our weak will freely turns from the good God toward inferior goods, seeking them inordinately for themselves in lieu of God. "When a will is made evil, what happens would not have happened, if the will had not wanted it to happen" (12, 8).

If our will does evil freely, our punishment is just. Our defects are evil because they deflect us from the Supreme Being to lesser beings. For example, greed or lust make us bad by acquiring good (gold or bodies) and sad by losing the better (God) (12, 9).

Our evil will starts an evil act "which is nothing but a weakening and worsening of the good in their nature." What makes our will evil? "An 'unmaking,' a defection from God. This very defection is deficient — in the sense of having no cause." Thus what made the angels bad was their falling away from the good will of God by their free choice.

Death is the ultimate punishment for sin (13, 4). And total death is when the soul abandons the body and God abandons the soul in hell. How can death be a punishment for sin when it happily releases saints into beatitude? And how can God punish with death those who have not sinned, or those who have been forgiven by grace? The martyrs' death is not a punishment, but rather a test of virtue and a happy door to eternal life.

> Mere physical death, the separation of soul and body that the dying must endure, is not good for anyone. For there is something harsh and unnatural in the violent sundering of what, in a living person, were closely linked and interwoven. And the experience lasts until there is a complete loss of all feeling that depends on the union of body and soul . . . However painful the sense of a dying person that all feeling is falling away, if it is suffered with faith and piety, it increases the merit of patience, without, however, forfeiting its claims to be called a punishment. (13, 6)

Although death is a punishment for sin, it can secure for the soul a grace that is security against all punishment for sin. "While men are in the throes of death and death is bringing on disintegration, death is good for no one, but it may become meritorious if suffered to retain or to gain some good." Being dead in itself is bad for the sinner, but good for the saints, the latter rejoicing, while the former head for eternal death (13, 8).

The condemnation of Adam was not only the deadly separation of soul and body, but also a second death, when soul and body are reunited in eternal punishment. Adam's sin and punishment are also passed down to us so that we his progeny, who were there in his loins when he sinned, are also corrupted and condemned. "We all existed in that one man, since, taken together, we were the one man who fell into sin through the woman who was made out of him before sin existed." Adam is Everyman, while Eve is Everywoman. And Everyman and Everywoman are soiled by sin, minideath and so destined to die.

In a sense, Adam and Eve's guilt anticipated their sin, since they were proud. For such "bad fruit" could only have come from a "bad tree" (14, 3). Augustine sees this pride as the foundation of the human city, while humility strongly builds up the city of God. "Whoever seeks to be more than he is, becomes less."

We should never, like the Manicheans, blame our bodies for our suffering. It is because we refused obedience to God that our bodies are weak and insubordinate.

> When people talk of the sufferings of the body, what they really mean are the sufferings of the soul which are felt in and because of the body . . . Pain of the body is simply the suffering of the soul arising from the body. It is, as it were, the soul's disapproval of what is happening to the body, much as that anguish of spirit which is called sorrow is a disapproval of what is happening in opposition to our wills. (14, 15)

Hence lust of the soul precedes bodily pleasures. Augustine makes much of the secret shame associated with carnal lusts.

Ultimate good is "the one by which goodness reaches its fullest consummation, while ultimate evil is that by which evil reaches the very heart of harm." Why does God allow evil? For example, why did he permit his angels to abandon him? "He (God) judged it better and more in accord with his power to bring some greater good even out of evil, than to permit no evil whatsoever" (22, 1).

Though God created all creatures good, "by choosing sin, such a nature brings evil on itself." Strangely enough, sin bears witness to the essential goodness of human nature. For otherwise falling away into darkness would not be a misfortune for nature. Sin is to nature as blindness is to the eye. For if we did not have the capacity to see, we would not miss it when our eyes become diseased. In like manner, sin deprives us of our happiness in God.

God made nature unfallen, "but free to fall away" and so to earn a punishment. "Yet he left our free choice unchecked because he foresaw to what good he would turn man's evil." Though many wicked people oppose him, God's wisdom and power are such that whatever appears to oppose him is turned to some good end or purpose which he foresaw to be good and holy.

Though some, such as Jung feel that Augustine diminishes the divine dualism of punishing and rewarding found in the Bible and the early Church Fathers in favor of his privation theory of evil,[1] he does show suffering as an important part of divine providence in testing and punishing men and women. For our weak and deficient wills cause evil in the world, either voluntary (sin) or involuntary (punishment for sin).

The inequalities of the world seem to be evil at first glance. However, when these sufferings are seen in the plenitude of the creative plan, they show a remarkable unity and beauty. We tend to concentrate on a tiny defective, suffering part of the universe without seeing its place

---

1. *Answer to Job.*

in the total picture of creation. For God uses our pains to correct earlier lapses, thus restoring world order. Neither sins nor suffering are necessary for the perfection of the universe, but souls which can sin if they wish are necessary. God in his providence draws good out of evil, which is better than not allowing the evil to exist at all.

Augustine's aesthetic view of the world and his privation theory of evil would set the pace for the medieval and renaissance evolution of the theology of sin and suffering. God sometimes allows suffering as a test of our faith. We will see what Augustine has to say about faith in the following chapter.

III.
UNDERSTAND IN ORDER TO BELIEVE
BELIEVE IN ORDER TO UNDERSTAND

(Sermon 43)

Augustine's Religious Experience [1]

When we study Augustine's theology of faith, we see that it reflects his own religious experience, his search for the truth and his conversion. He soon tired of Manicheanism and the Academy and finally found in Neoplatonism a line of thought that appeared to be true. Like Clement of Alexandria, Augustine believed that there was some of God's truth in the writings of pagan authors. The Neoplatonists inspired Augustine to begin his long ascent to the Truth with the aid of faith and reason. Thus he writes against the Academics: "After many centuries and much contention, a philosophy has finally been evolved which, in my opinion, is entirely true. It is not limited to this world, . . . it reveals another, the intelligible world" (3, 19).

Neoplatonism gave Augustine his solution to the problem of evil, releasing him from the materialism of Manicheanism and showing him that evil is really the privation of the good. Moreover, Neoplatonism helped him to see the wisdom of the gospel approach to spirituality. Deeply impressed by the conversion of the Neoplatonist, Victorinus, Augustine made his own voluntary, loving ascent to Christ in 387 following the intellectual preparation of Neoplatonism.[2]

---

1. This chapter appeared earlier as chapter three of *Dimensions of Faith* (Chicago: Loyola University Press, 1969).
2. See F. Copleston, *A History of Philosophy*, vol. II, pt. I (Garden City: Doubleday, 1962), 56-57, 63.

27

Faith and Reason

The problem of faith and reason interested Augustine. Though he had sought the truth through reason, it was through reason enlightened by faith that he was to find it. Never separating faith and reason as has been done in modern times, Augustine rather tried to penetrate by his understanding the Christian faith and to see the world and human life in the light of Christian wisdom. Reason helps to bring one to faith, and once he has the gift of faith, reason helps him to penetrate the truths of his belief. Based on his own experience, Augustine writes concerning the *True Religion* that reason helped him to understand what he believed, just as it aided him on his way to faith (24, 45).

Augustine does not split man and woman into the natural and supernatural, but treats them as they really are, that is, with a supernatural end. Augustine is always interested in man and woman in their concrete relationships with God here and now. Perhaps we could describe the Christian philosophy of Augustine as our rational contemplation of Christian revelation, faith seeking understanding.

Faith and reason aid each other in the pursuit of Christian wisdom. Reason plays an important role in faith for it is only reasoning, thinking creatures, such as man and woman who can believe. Understand in order to believe, believe in order to understand. Augustine explains the cooperation of faith and reason in human conversion in one of his sermons (S 43).

> From one aspect he is right when he says, "May I understand in order to believe." And I am right when I say with the Prophet, "Believe in order that you may understand." We both speak the truth and agree. Therefore, understand in order that you may believe; believe in order that you may understand. Briefly I explain how we can accept each other's opinion without controversy. Understand my word in order that you may believe. Believe God's word in order that you may understand.

Understand my word that you should believe. This is the reasonable affirmation of the authority upon which faith is based. Certainly the authoritative words and example of Ambrose and Victorinus led Augustine to believe, but not without divine guidance. Faith is reasonable for no one believes unless first he or she thinks it should be believed.[1]

Which comes first, faith or reason? As we have seen, Augustine does not clearly separate the two. Each aids the other on the road to

---

1. *Predestination of the Saints* 2, 5.

beatitude. "Therefore, it is reasonable that in great things which cannot be grasped, faith precedes reason. Of course, the reason, however small, which precedes this, antecedes faith" (L 120) (F). Reason somehow precedes faith, for only a rational person can believe. Thus the intellect must be capable of accepting the reasonable authority on which faith is based. "Unless a man understands something, he cannot believe God. Nevertheless, by the very faith by which he believes, he is restored that he may understand more" (On Ps 118:18, 3) (N).

Faith and reason work together, faith perfecting reason, leading it to further understanding. By our faith our eyes are opened so that reason, purified by faith, can seek the truth. Faith builds on reason, elevating it so that one may attain the heights of understanding. Christ promised that those who believed in him would see.

What does he promise to believers, brothers? You will know the truth. What? Had they not known it when the Lord spoke? If they did not know, how did they believe? We believe in order to know, we do not know in order to believe. What we will know, "Eye has not seen . . ." (Is 64:4; 1 Cor 2:9). (On Jn 40:9) (N)

Faith is the necessary prelude to a partial understanding of revealed truths here below and the full vision of eternity.

Should we just accept revelation on faith alone without in any way seeking to understand what we believe? Augustine replies, "Then you must revise your rule, not indeed to the extent of throwing your faith overboard, but to allow you to bring the light of reason to bear on what you already hold firmly by faith" (L 120).

In his commentary on John (tr. 27, 7) Augustine notes that Jesus told his disciples that some of them did not believe (cf. Jn 6:60, 72), and so they could not understand. "They understand not, because they believe not" (Is 7:9).

"If you do not believe, you will not understand," for we who are united by faith are quickened by understanding. First we believe and then we can be quickened by understanding. For if we adhere to faith, we will not resist.

The resister blocks the light of faith, shutting off his mind. "Let them believe and open, let them open and be illumined." Jesus knew which of his disciples believed and which did not. Moreover, he told them that no one could come to him unless it was by means of the Father's gift of faith.

Augustine comments (tr. 36, 7), "Let him who can, understand; let him who cannot understand believe." Jesus said that he is not alone, but with his Father who sent him (Jn 8:15-18). But, if the Father is with him, how has he sent him? How can Christ be both here and there? How is this to be believed, how apprehended?

"For that very reason it is right to believe, because it is not immediately to be apprehended." If the truth were quickly grasped, there would be no need to believe it, since it would already be seen.

> It is because you do not apprehend that you believe. But by believing you are capable of apprehending. For if you do not believe, you will never apprehend, since you will remain less capable. Let faith, then, purify you, that understanding may fill you.

Jesus is with his Father who sent him. "So I see, so I understand, in short, so I believe; in case it may smack of arrogance, so I understand." Jesus was here in the flesh and he is here now in his Godhead. He was both with his Father and had not left his Father.

Faith seeking understanding is a good epitome of Augustine's theology of faith. Faith, under the guidance of Christ, has a tension for understanding, which will be complete only in the future vision.

Is the faith of Augustine a prelude to understanding in the Manichean sense, where the simple faith of the hearers was looked down upon as inferior to the superior gnosis of the elect? Augustine's faith is a necessary prerequisite to understanding, but it continues to work along with reason. Augustine's gnosis is a cooperative effort of God and man. God further enlightens the believer so that he can partially understand the revealed truths and eventually be united with Truth himself in the everlasting vision.

Thinking with Assent

Augustine, reflecting the rapport between faith and reason, describes the act of faith as "thinking with assent."

> To believe is nothing more than to think with assent. Not everyone who thinks, believes, since many think in order not to believe. But everyone who believes, thinks. Believing, he thinks; and thinking, he believes.[1]

While in his *Confessions* (10, 11) Augustine describes *cogitatio* (thinking) as a bringing together (*cogere*) of things hidden in the

---

1. *Predestination of the Saints* 2, 5.

memory, in his treatise on *The Trinity* (1, 15) (F) he calls thinking a restless turning over of things in the mind. Augustine's assent of faith, resembling that of Clement of Alexandria,[1] was not just an intellectual acceptance, but involved the whole person in a judgment of the truth and goodness of the object. So the affective power plays an important role in Augustine's faith.

In Augustine's act of belief, the thinking precedes the assent. This mirrors his own experience, for he thought long and hard before he finally assented to Christ. However, the thinking does not cease with the assent, but continues along with it, using reason perfected by faith in order to search for the understanding of the things believed. Both the intellectual and the affective powers cooperate in Augustine's faith quest for the true and good God.

Affective Faith

Augustine's theory of morality stressed the affective side, reflecting the gospels and Neoplatonism.[2] Love played an important role in his own conversion. From his own experience he knew that one can easily turn from God to the love of creatures or he can turn toward the good God in loving faith. Through faith one seeks the beatifying vision of Truth, but he or she seeks it willingly and rejoices in him in charity (On Jn 26, 44). In order for faith to be a virtue, it must somehow act in the order of love.[3]

Following the Neoplatonic line, Augustine taught the primacy of the will in human knowledge. What is known cannot be divorced from what is loved, since all cognition is somehow dependent on interest. Nothing is fully known without the consent of the will. Complete cognition lies with affection. Hence the recognition of Christ through faith is primarily a movement of the will. It is true that reason takes in and knows reality, both eternal and temporal. But since reason is primarily passive and neutral, it must be directed to recognize what it does not recognize by the will. It is the will which needs cleansing by faith in order to command the recognition of Christ.[4]

God must be primarily in the will, not the intellect, for the intellect is under the will. In faith we conform our will to God's. Without faith

---

1. *Stromata* 7, 10. See also H. Wolfson, *The Philosophy of the Church Fathers* (Cambridge: Harvard University Press, 1956), 129.
2. Copleston, *A History of Philosophy* II, I, 74, 94.
3. *Morals of the Catholic Church* 1, 5.
4. See R. Cushman, "Faith and Reason in the Thought of Augustine," in *Church History* XIX, 1950, 274, 285.

we do not recognize God because we do not love him. Men and women use the divine light for science, but do not recognize the light. Blinded by their perverted wills, and refusing to submit to the inward illuminator, the Platonists turned outwards to nature in search of God. It was love and desire that they lacked, namely the love and desire that turns diffused awareness into true cognition (*The Trinity* 9, 12).

Augustine saw the function of love in his own conversion. Although his intellect had knowledge of the gospels, yet it was his will that was moved through the gift of faith. In contrast with Aristotle for whom appetite follows intellect, Augustine taught that in knowledge as well as in faith, love precedes.[1] So desire spurs us on to an awareness of God. However, since the will is perverse, we turn from the divine light to creatures illuminated by the light. And there follows an immoderate love of the senses, pride and self-love.

Christ enlightens us, healing our sick will. Curing our blindness, he awakens us so that we can recognize God. Freeing us from our inordinate love for material things and from self-love, Christ moves our will through faith so that we can love the good, of which we are aware without acknowledging it. Thus humbled and purified by faith, we consent to the Truth and the Good (*The Trinity* 4, 18).

If we wish to understand correctly the sense of faith seeking understanding in Augustine, we should see how charity or love plays an important role in each aspect of inquiring faith. Reason seeking understanding, seeking greater purity and union with God, is voluntarily subordinated to him and in charity rejoices in him.[2]

Augustine teaches a threefold belief, namely: to believe God (*credere Deo*), to believe God (*credere Deum*), and to believe in God (*credere in Deum*). The first is to believe that God speaks the truth; the second is to believe that he is God, while the third is to love him.[3] It is in the third part of the threefold *credere* that the living, loving faith of the believer is found.

Commenting on John 6:29, Augustine writes, "This is the work of God, that you believe in him whom he has sent" (29, 7). Not everyone who believes God believes in him. For example, the demons believed him, but did not believe in him. "What is it to believe in him? Believing, to love; believing, to prize him highly; believing, to go to him and be incorporated in his members." This is the faith acting through love described by the apostle (Gal 5:6). The difference between the faith of the unholy people and that of the elect is love (S 158). Augustine in one of his sermons (S 40) exhorts his flock to charity

---

1. *Ibid.*, 287-89.
2. See R. Holte, "*Béatitude et Sagesse, Saint Augustin et le Problème de la Fin de L'homme dans la Philosophie Ancienne*", Paris, *Etudes Augustiniennes*, 1962, 385.
3. *Sermon on the Creed; On Psalm* 77, 8; *On John* 29, 6.

rather than to faith, for if they have charity and love, they will have faith. For Augustine to believe in Christ is the belief of supernatural love, charity.

The Light of Faith

Augustine taught an illumination theory of knowledge, rooted in Christian tradition and reflecting Plato and Plotinus. It is the divine light in whom and by whom and through whom all those things which are luminous to the intellect become luminous.[1] For Plotinus the One God is the transcendent light, illuminating the human minds. Augustine's theory of divine illumination means an intuition of direct, immediate contact and participation in the divine light.[2]

Why did Augustine teach divine illumination? Because the human mind is changeable and temporal and so needs help to see the unchangeable and eternal truths (On Ps 119:4). Only changeless Truth himself can illuminate us so that we can see. The divine light enables us to see the relationship of temporal things to the eternal truths. By it we can see the true meaning of creation, the world sustained, sanctified and recreated by the Word Incarnate, in whose image it was made.[3]

Augustine compared the divine illumination of the soul to the light of the sun in the visible world. The sun, created facsimile of the divine light, shines on the visible world, enabling the eye to see. In a similar manner, God enlightens the mind, the eye of the soul, with an incorporeal light (*The Trinity* 12, 15).

Can one make use of this divine light outside of faith? Yes, he or she must in order to perceive the eternal truths. So the Platonists used the divine light, but they did not recognize it. There is a wide gulf between being enlightened by God, and acknowledging the light. Though God is used by many, he is only recognized by the few who go inside themselves to discover the source of the light, the author and exemplar of the world, the Word Incarnate. It is only by faith that we can recognize the divine light and seek the beatifying union with the source of the light.

Augustine taught the purifying effects of the divine light, reflecting

---

1. *Soliloquies* 1, 8, 15; *City of God* 11, 10.
2. See C. Schuetzinger, *German Controversy on St. Augustine's Illumination Theory* (New York: Pageant, 1960), 79. See also Gilson, *The Christian Philosophy of Saint Augustine* 79, 92; Holte *"Béatitude et Sagesse"*, 313ff.
3. *City of God* 8, 6; *The Trinity* 12, 14; Cushman, *Faith and Reason in the Thought of Saint Augustine* 277, 278.

the gospels and Plotinus. The sick mind, the eye of the soul loving the darkness, is healed by the light of faith which cleanses it of earthly desires.[1] As in Plotinus, so in Augustine the purification line is the reverse of the illumination line, culminating in union with the One, the Good, the source of the light. In Augustine illumination and purification seem to be simultaneous, for we are purified by the divine light. As the light intensifies, we are drawn into union with the source of the light. Union can be temporary as in mystical experiences or eternal in the next life. The illumination, purification, union line of Plato, Plotinus and Augustine led the way for future developments in mystical theology.[2]

It is the healing light of faith that begins our road to union and vision.

> Faith precedes reason, it cleanses the heart that it may bear the light of greater reason. Therefore, it is reasonably said by the prophet, "Unless you believe, you will not understand" (Is 7:9). In discerning these two, he meant that we believe so that we may be able to understand that which we believe. (L 120)

Belief is a necessary prelude to the partial understanding on earth and the full vision of eternity. With our minds purified by faith, we are free to go on to vision and union with divine Truth. "Unless we walk by faith, we shall not be able to reach that vision which passes not, but abides, that vision which comes from our being fastened to truth by a purified mind" (*Christian Doctrine* 2, 12) (F).

Eschatology of Faith

Faith begins our ascent to the Truth which culminates in beatifying union. Augustine, following the lead of scriptures, taught an eschatological faith. Quoting the Epistle to the Hebrews, he wrote of faith as the assurance of the things to be hoped for and the conviction of things not yet seen (*Enchiridion* 1, 18). Augustine clearly taught the rapport between faith and vision. Faith is like the foundation of a house, or the root of a tree. The beautiful tree of beatitude grows from the humble root of faith (On Jn 40:8). Although the foundation of a house and the root of a tree are not pleasing to the eye, yet they have a necessary rapport with their attractive fulfillment. So humble faith

---

1. *Soliloquies* 1, 14; *City of God* 11, 2.
2. See J. Pieper, *Scholasticism* (London: Faber and Faber, 1960), 51.

is the foundation, the beginning of eternal life. It is the root which will flower into beatitude.

Confessions: Story of Faith

Augustine's *Confessions* give us a good meditative account of his own faith history and conversion. When he wrote, "Understand in order to believe; believe in order to understand," he may well have been thinking of himself and how he had studied Plotinus and read the gospels and listened to Ambrose, Alpius and Nebridius. "Understand in order to believe." After his conversion, he sought understanding through faith. "Believe in order to understand."

Augustine himself experienced the way of illumination, purgation and union. With God's help he was cleansed from sin and earthly desires. By the grace of God, he experienced a conversion, with the purifying light drawing him toward union with the source of the light, the one, true and good God.

The I-Thou theme of the *Confessions* illustrates Augustine's striving for union. "You have made us for yourself, and our heart is restless until it rests in you" (*Confessions* 1, 1). Since his faith represented security of mind and heart for which he had struggled so long, he now felt the need to communicate his experience to others seeking the same beatitude.

The Law of Works and the Law of Faith

Although in his earlier works he had emphasized the part of man in the act of faith, in his later anti-Pelagian writings Augustine stresses man's total dependence on God for the gift of faith. In his *On The Spirit and the Letter* (412) Augustine is strongly Pauline in opposing the law of faith to the law of boastful works. We are justified "not by the law of works, but by the law of faith; not by the letter, but by the spirit; not by merits of deeds, but by free grace" (22). Our righteousness is entirely from God, for if it is by the works of the law, Christ died in vain. By our faith in Jesus Christ we obtain salvation, both as it is begun in us and insofar as its fulfillment is awaited in hope (51). Let the fearful soul flee to the mercy of God, whose grace through the Holy Spirit causes the soul to delight in his teaching more than in that which opposes. Our will to believe is entirely from God, who aids us both internally and externally.

In his *Predestination of the Saints* (428-29) Augustine answers the Semipelagians, insisting that even the beginning of faith is from God, for "what have you that you have not received?" (1 Cor 4:7). We are not justified by our own good works, but by faith, for "faith itself is given first, from which may be obtained other things, which are especially characterized as works in which man may live righteously" (12). Although Cornelius gave alms and prayed before he believed in Christ, he could not have done this without some faith, for the Lord not only builds the spiritual edifice, but he also digs the foundation.

Surely all deserve condemnation; therefore, the gift of faith is from God's bountiful mercy and should be received with gratitude. Why God predestines some and not others is his own secret. This we know: the elect are not chosen because they have believed, but in order that they might believe. "Yon have not chosen me, but I have chosen you" (Jn 15:16). Before the beginning of the world, God predestined those whom he would elect. "Thus God elected believers, but he chose them that they might be so, not because they were already so" (34).

Our faith is God's gift, but so also are our works of justice which are the fruit of our faith (S 49). It is difficult to live badly if we believe well. We should believe with our whole heart, without hesitation or suspicion.

Fides (faith) has two syllables, the first from a deed and the second from a word. When Augustine asks his people if they believe, they respond, "We believe." If we do what we say, it is faith. Although Augustine can hear their response, he cannot see into their hearts.

A Summary of Augustine's Theology of Faith

Augustine's whole life had been a search for the Truth, first as a student of Manicheanism, then as an Academic and as a Neoplatonist. But it is only through faith that he was to find Christ, God's begotten truth, the cause and exemplar of all true things.

Augustine taught the close rapport between faith and reason. "Understand in order to believe; believe in order to understand." Faith leads to an understanding of the things that we believe. Yet somehow reason precedes faith, for one must understand something in order to believe. Faith is "thinking with assent" in which reason strives to see the unseen Truth, while at the same time giving firm assent.

Wisdom combines faith and reason (Ps 135). "His saints are spiritual men, to whom he has given not only to believe, but also to understand things divine." However, those who have not attained this and only hold firmly onto their faith are called of the earth. "Wisdom is the knowledge and love of that which is eternal and abides unchangeable, namely, God" (*Expositions on Psalm 135*).

Often our assent of faith is defective because of our sick wills. So we cannot turn from the love of creatures to the love of their Creator. It is the affective belief in God, inspired by charity, that separates the believers from the unholy people.

Augustine's faith is a divine illumination reflecting the gospels and Neoplatonism. Christ, God's truth Incarnate, illumines the soul in the light of faith, purifying the heart that it may bear the light of greater reason, drawing the believer into union with the source of the light. By the divine light one cannot only see the eternal truths, but also recognize the light as from God, and perceive in the world the reflections of the divine ideas according to which they were made. Far from separating us from the world, faith aids us to see its true image and end, divine Truth.

Finally, faith is all from God, not in any way due to our own good works. Even its beginning is from God who from all eternity has predestined the faithful, not because they have believed, but in order that they might believe.

For Augustine to believe in God is to love God. In the following chapter we will see the development of his Neoplatonic theology of love.

IV.
LATE HAVE I LOVED YOU

(Confessions 10, 27)

As we have seen, the Alexandrian Plotinus introduced Plato's *eros* or love to the West with an overlay of the mystery religions. The Alexandrian school of Platonism had sought to reconcile the dualism of God and matter with intermediaries. As the soul had descended from God into matter, now it wants to return to him.

Like his mentor Plato, Plotinus teaches that the soul pursues beauty, whose reflection is seen in earthly beauty.

> So divine and precious is the soul, be confident that by its power you can attain divinity. Start your ascent. You will not need to search long. Few are the steps that separate you from your goal. Take as your guide the most divine part of the soul, that which borders on the superior realm from which it comes. (*Enneads* 5, 1, 10)

It is eros which gives the soul its upward drive toward the heavenly. With the aid of eros the soul rises toward the Beautiful, reversing the order of descent. For Plotinus, God is eros. Not only is he worthy of love, but he is love itself and he is Beauty itself, the object of all love (6, 8, 15).

Augustine, Philosopher of Love [1]

It is Augustine, student of Plotinus, who is the great psychologist and theologian of love in the West and who has been credited with synthesizing Neoplatonic *eros* with Christian *agape* (love), thus combining descent and ascent in *caritas*.

---

1. This chapter first appeared in *Dimensions of Love* (Garden City: Doubleday, 1975).

Let us see something of love in Augustine's early works (386-390), when his Neoplatonism is still fresh. As time passed, he became less philosophical and more scriptural with more emphasis on God's grace.

One of the favorite topics of the philosophers is happiness. For all agree that people want to be happy. The big question is, what is happiness? This was a natural for Augustine and his friends in their discussions at Cassiciacum. Their conversations in *The Happy Life* (386) comprise Augustine's first completed work at the age of thirty-two.

Like many young men, Augustine had searched for happiness in various philosophies, that is, Manicheanism, the Academy and Platonism. He groped for it in his thirteen years of common law marriage and in his career as a rhetor. But none of these were satisfying. He concludes that God is the only true source of lasting happiness. Though we are drawn to God, we are held back by earthly attractions.

As long as we are still seeking and not yet satiated by the fountain itself—to use our word—by fullness, we must confess that we have not yet reached our measure. Therefore, notwithstanding the help of God, we are not yet wise and happy. (4, 35) (F)

While at Cassiciacum he also wrote his *Soliloquies,* a dialogue with himself on the knowledge of God and the soul. We can know God through our study of the soul which is made in his image. This is Augustine's first mention of a psychological approach to God, which would culminate in his *Trinity.* Since the soul must resemble its Creator, why not study it as a way to God?

Augustine wants to know God and the soul which he loves. But his reason asks whether he does not know something like God. Augustine replies, "If I knew anything like God, I would doubtless love it. But up to now I love nothing except God and the soul, neither of which I know" (*Soliloquies* 1, 2) (F).

But does not Augustine love his friends? Yes, "because they have rational souls, which I love even in thieves . . . And so I love my friends all the more, the better use they make of the rational soul. Or at least according to the manner in which they desire to use it well" (1, 2). Augustine's view of reason as the divine and loveable part of us reflects a major trend in Hellenistic philosophy.

Although Augustine loves his friends and knows them superficially—that is, by the senses, he does not yet know them interiorly.

The law of friendship is most just by which it is ordained that we should love a friend neither less nor more than we love ourselves. Accordingly, since I do not know myself, what shame can I possibly inflict on a friend when I say he is unknown to me, especially when I believe that he himself does not know himself? (1, 3)

Augustine teaches the Platonic precedence of love in cognition, a keen insight which would be rediscovered by modern philosophers, educators and psychologists.

Are there lesser loves than the love of God? Yes, the love of friends, health, wealth, honors, wife, etc. However, all of these loves are undermined by the fear of loss, for friends depart, health weakens, money is lost, dishonor comes, a wife dies.

So Augustine pursues divine love. "And this boon grows on me day by day, for the more my hope increases of seeing that Beauty which I so long for, the more is all my love and delight turned toward him" (1, 10).

Augustine is sometimes accused of having a negative view of sex. But he speaks as a man of experience, for he had the pleasures of sexual intercourse for many years. But it was a joy that he found to be ephemeral. Augustine is often the *bête noire* for the proponents of free sexual love. However, his main point is often missed, namely, that this is not the highest form of love.

In 388 at Rome Augustine begins his role as the defender of his new faith against the Manicheans, portraying the "morals of the Catholic Church" as superior to those of the heretics.

Taking up the theme of *The Happy Life* and the *Soliloquies,* he claims that happiness is the enjoyment of our own chief good, which cannot be lost except by the action of our own free will. We cannot be happy unless we possess what we love. For if we desire something unattainable, love something hurtful or possess something that we do not love, we are unhappy.

What is happiness, then? It is having one's chief loved good at hand. Our main good cannot be inferior to us, or we also will become inferior.[1] And human love always carries with it the risk of loss. So what remains? "God then remains, in following after whom we live both well and happily" (7).

Both the Old and New Testaments teach love. "If then to those who love God all things issue in good, and if, as no one doubts, the chief and perfect good is not only to be loved, but to be loved so that nothing shall be loved better" our chief good must be God and no one but ourselves can separate us from him (11).

It is Christ, love incarnate, and his Spirit who unite us to God. Why?

---

1. "Morals of the Catholic Church," 3-4, in *The Basic Writings of Saint Augustine* (New York: Random House, 1948), 323.

Because through love we become conformed to Christ by the Holy Spirit.

Augustine is writing on the morals of the Catholic Church. But morality is virtue and virtue is love.

> As to virtue leading us to a happy life, I hold virtue to be nothing else than perfect love of God . . . Temperance is love giving itself entirely to that which is loved; fortitude is love readily bearing all things for the sake of the loved object; justice is love serving only the loved object, and, therefore, ruling rightly; prudence is love distinguishing with sagacity between what hinders it and what helps it. (11)

The object of love is God, so that temperance keeps whole and entire for God, fortitude bears everything for God, etc. (15).

We have been talking about love of God, around which the whole of Christian morality revolves. But what of love of self and neighbor? First Augustine explains self-love. "It is impossible for one who loves God not to love himself. For he alone has a proper love for himself, who aims diligently at the attainment of the chief and true good" — God.

Moreover, we should show our love for our neighbor by trying to draw him or her to the same highest good which we are pursuing. Both divine love and neighborly love are first in their own way. Thus the love of God is first in beginning, while love of neighbor is first in coming to perfection (26). Augustine then concludes with examples of Christian anchorites and cenobites and others living in perfect charity.

Augustine's dialogue *On Music* was started in 387, before his conversion, and was finished in 391. It is one of his treatises on the liberal arts. In the sixth book on the hierarchy of numbers he speaks of delight (*delectatio*) in parallel terms to love. "For delight is a kind of weight (*pondus*) in the soul. Therefore delight orders the soul." Thus we should order ourselves between the higher and the lower, avoiding the troubles of the lower and taking delight in the higher (6, 11). Delight, like love, is a weight bearing us toward the object of our love, as the heft of a stone carries it down to the earth or the light weight of a flame rises up to the heights.[1]

Everybody loves beautiful things. But improper love turns us away from God.

> Then the love of acting on the stream of its bodily passions turns the soul away from the contemplation of eternal things, diverting

---

1. See also *Confessions* 13, 9; *The City of God* 11, 28.

its attention with the care of sensible pleasure. It does this with reacting numbers. But the love of operating on bodies also turns it away, and makes it restless. This it does with advancing numbers . . . But the general love of action, turning away from the true, arises from pride by which vice the soul has preferred imitating God to serving him. (6, 13) (F)

The soul is nothing of itself, but is from God. By staying in order it is quickened in mind and conscience by the presence of God. However, puffed with pride, it is out of synch, disordered, goes out empty, and becomes less and less, putting itself away from God.

It is the love of lower beauty which soils the soul, causing disorder. "That soul keeps order, that, with its whole self, loves him above itself, that is, God, and fellow souls as itself. In virtue of this love, it orders lower things and suffers no disorder from them" (6, 14). "And so let us put our joy neither in carnal pleasure, nor in honors and praises or other, nor in the exploring of things touching the body from without, having God within where all we love is sure and unchangeable."

Delight in music and in love are proper orderings. So when things get out of order in the musical world — cacophony. Dissonance and lack of harmony can be found both in music and in love.

Pastor of Love

In his priestly years — from 391 onward — Augustine is less philosophical and more pastoral in tone, beginning with his *Confessions* (397), written to help others to find their way along his pathway of love, others who are trapped in the same *culs-de-sac* of earthly delights which he had fallen into.

Augustine's *Confessions* are a song of love. "For love of your love I perform this task" (11, 1).[1] Since we are made for God, our love will not be sated until it possesses our beloved. "Our heart is restless until it rests in you" (1, 1).

In reviewing his early life Augustine regrets some of his young loves for play, sex, honor and power — all lower loves. "These lower goods have their delights, but none such as my God, who has made all things, for in him the just man finds delight and he is the joy of the upright heart" (2, 5).

Augustine is a man of many loves. Besides his youthful lusts, his

---

1. *Confessions*, J. Ryan, tr. (Garden City: Doubleday, 1960).

filial love of Monica, his paternal affection for Adeodatus and his sexual love for his anonymous consort, he also enjoyed the love of friendship. However, he saw all of these loves end in death. For friendship unites two souls into one, which is destined to be split. At the sudden death of a close friend, Augustine cries out, "I marveled that other men should live, because he whom I had loved as if he should never die was dead" (4, 6). With half of his soul gone, Augustine feels that his portion may depart also.

> Human friendship and love, though great, are ephemeral. But blessed is the man who loves you and his friend in you, and his enemy for your sake. For he alone loses no dear one to whom all are dear in him who is not lost. But who is this unless our God, the God who made heaven and earth and fills all things because by filling them he made them. (4, 9)

The divine light illumines his friendship. "You beat back my feeble sight, sending down your beams most powerfully upon me, and I trembled with love and awe" (7, 10).

Augustine is not a pessimist or an exaggerated dualist, seeing material things as evil, as the Manicheans did. No, all things are created good. However, they are corruptible and so tend to lose their goodness. They must be good in the beginning for otherwise they would not be corruptible. All of these things in their goodness reflect and praise their Creator, the highest and incorruptible good (7, 12).

What is evil? It is the disordered love which centers on lower goods in lieu of the higher. "It is the perversity of will, twisted away from the supreme substance, yourself, O God, and toward lower things" (7, 10). Though he is borne down by the weight of carnal lust, there still remains in Augustine a remembrance of God.

Augustine had many loves. But how does the love of God compare with these? "Not with doubtful, but with sure knowledge do I love you, O Lord. By your word have you transfixed my heart, and I have loved you, O Lord. Heaven and earth and all things in them, behold! Everywhere they say to me that I should love you."

It is not beautiful bodies, or temporal fame, or shining lights, or sweet songs, delightful flowers or shapely legs.

> Yet I do love a certain light, a certain voice, a certain color, a certain food, a certain embrace, when I love my God. A light, a voice, an odor, a food, an embrace for the man within me, where his light, which no place can contain, floods my soul; where he utters his words that time does not speed away; where he sends forth an aroma that no mind can scatter; where he provides food

that no eating can lessen; where he so clings that satiety does not sunder us. This is what I love when I love my God. (10, 6)

For thirty-two years Augustine had pursued mortal beauties until at last he had found Beauty itself.

Too late have I loved you, O Beauty, so ancient and so new. Too late have I loved you! Behold you were within me, while I was outside. It was there that I sought you, and, a deformed creature, rushed headlong upon these things of beauty which you have made. You were with me, but I was not with you. They kept me far from you, those fair things which, if they were not in you, would not exist at all.
You have called to me, and have cried out, and have shattered my deafness. You have blazed forth with light, and have shone upon me, and you have put my blindness to flight! You have sent forth fragrance, and I have drawn in my breath, and I pant after you. I have tasted you and I hunger and thirst for you. You have touched me and I have burned for your peace. (10, 27)

It is the weight (*pondus*) of his love that moves Augustine toward God, where he will find rest. As fire rises and stones fall, as oil floats and water sinks until they find their place of natural rest, so "my love is my weight. I am borne about by it, wheresoever I am borne. By your gift I am enkindled, and we are carried upwards. We glow with inner fire and we go on. We ascend steps within the heart and we sing a gradual psalm" (13, 9). But this weighty love is not something that we have acquired. No, it is God's gratuitous gift to us.

After he was consecrated bishop of Hippo in 395, Augustine's philosophy of love took on a more pastoral hue. For example, in 399 he writes to encourage his catechists in their sometimes discouraging work.

The first aim of the catechist should be to teach his disciples that Christ came to instruct us in love. Why else did Christ come than to manifest God's love for us sinners and to give us an example to love each other?

Even if at first we found it irksome to love him, now at least it should not prove irksome to return that love. For there is nothing that invites love more than to be beforehand in loving. And that heart is overhard which even though it were unwilling to bestow love, would be unwilling to return it.
There is no greater reason either for the birth or growth of love than when one who as yet does not love, perceives that he is

loved. Or when he who loves already hopes either that he may yet be loved in return, or actually has proof that he is loved. (4, 7) (A)

If this is true in natural passions, how much more so in friendship. "For what else do we have to be on our guard against in an offense against friendship than that our friend should think that we do not love him, or that we love him less than he loves us." If a friend finds out that we love him less, will not his affection cool, especially if it is of the utilitarian type?

Though love of friendship is great when traded on an equal basis, the love of a superior for an inferior is even greater. "For love is more welcome when it is not burnt up by the drought of want, but issues forth from the overflowing stream of beneficence. For the former springs from misery, while the latter arises from commiseration."

This is the love of God which Christ came to teach us. Christ came chiefly that man might learn how much God loves him, and might learn this to the end that he might begin to glow with love of him by whom he was first loved, and so might love his neighbor at the bidding and after the example of him who made himself man's neighbor by loving him, when instead of being his neighbor, he was wandering far from him. (4, 8)

This is the epitome of the scriptures and of all catechizing, as well, namely, that God loved us first and that we should love him in return (5, 9).

Love is most important in Christian teaching, Augustine writes (394-426). He distinguishes two types of love, *frui* and *uti* (enjoyment and use). The things of the world are to be used to bring us to our final end. "But because of their eagerness to enjoy the creature in place of the Creator, men have been conformed to the world and have fittingly been called 'the world' " (1, 12) (F). The enjoyment of temporal things does not lead to happiness since there is a constant risk of loss. The enjoyment of eternal things alone can bring true happiness (1, 22).

But what about human love, *frui* or *uti*?
We have been commanded to love one another. But the question is whether man is to be loved by man for his own sake or for another reason. If he is loved for his own sake, we are enjoying him (*frui*). However, if he is loved for another reason, we are using him (*uti*). (1, 22)

Augustine prefers *uti* to *frui* in the case of human beings and other creatures. Thus we should use our love of our friends to help us reach God.

> The same is true of our self-love.
> No one ought to enjoy himself, if you observe clearly, because he should not love himself for his own sake, but because of him whom he ought to enjoy . . . If he loves himself for his own sake, he does not refer himself to God. But since he has turned to himself, he is not turned toward something unchangeable.

We cannot enjoy ourselves perfectly, for God is the only one in whom we can find total delight. "Therefore, if you ought to love yourself, not for your own sake, but on account of him who is the most fitting object of your love, no other man should be angered if you love him also for the sake of God."

So one should love his neighbor with reference to God. "Thus loving him as himself, he refers all love of himself and the other to that love of God which suffers no trickle to be led off from itself by those whose diversion its own volume might lessen."

There are four things to be loved. Things above, ourselves, things equal to ourselves and things below. We do not have to worry about the second and the fourth, since we all love ourselves and our own bodies (1, 23). We exist between God and creatures. So it is most unjust for us to expect lower creatures to serve us, if we, in turn, refuse to serve God.

Though we do not need to be reminded to love ourselves or our bodies, we must be prompted to love God and our neighbor.

> Now the purpose of this charge is charity, a twofold love of God and neighbor . . . Since the love of God has precedence, and since the measure of that love has been so defined that all other loves are to fuse in him, it seems that no mention has been made about love of ourselves. (1, 26)

But we should love our neighbor as ourselves.

The just and holy person "has a well-regulated love and neither loves what he ought not to, nor fails to love what he should" (1, 27). Sinners as sinners should not be loved. Man and woman is loved for God and God for his own sake.

> And if God is to be loved more than any man, each one ought to love God more than himself. Thus another man should be

loved more than our own bodies, because all those things are to be loved for the sake of God.

Another person can enjoy God with us, whereas our body cannot. All people should be loved equally. But is there not a hierarchy of love among persons? One must decide who is more in need (1, 28).

How should we act who are united by the love of God, the enjoyment of whom constitutes our happy life and from whom all who love him receive their existence and their love of him? He wants us to love in order to share his love with us, rewarding us with himself, the object of our love. So we even love our enemies in compassion since they have removed themselves from the reward of divine love (1, 29).

However, the big question still remains, namely, how can God love us? The pagan gods had no need of human beings and so did not love them. "How does God love us? If he enjoys us, he needs a benefit that is ours, something no sane man would say, because he himself is our every good or else it comes from him."

If God, then, does not love us for enjoyment (*frui*), does he do so with the love of use (*uti*)? Augustine replies, "If he neither enjoys us nor uses us, I cannot discover how he loves us" (1, 31). However, the use God makes of us is not the same way we use creation in order to help our ultimate enjoyment of God. "God refers that use which he is said to make of us for our benefit, not to his benefit, but only to his goodness." For we exist only because of the superabundance of his goodness (1, 32).

For Augustine *caritas* (love or charity) and *cupiditas* (lust) are exact opposites. Thus "charity is a motion of the soul whose purpose is to enjoy God for his own sake and oneself and one's neighbor for the sake of God," whereas *cupiditas* is enjoying oneself, neighbor or any other creature without any reference to God.

Unbridled lust in ourselves is vice, while aimed at others it is crime. Charity, on the other hand, used for oneself is utility, whereas for another it is kindness. "The more the power of lust is destroyed, the more the power of charity is strengthened" (3, 10).

In conclusion, love is the central message of the scriptures. So when one becomes a Christian, he should do so out of love for God, who has loved him first through his Son, Jesus Christ.

Augustine's many pastoral sermons also reflect his concern for love. For example, in Sermon 21 he comments on Psalm 63:11, "The just man will rejoice in the Lord." Love is based on hope.

You love money, but you would not love it if you did not hope. You love your wife, not already wed, but about to be wed.

> Perhaps your beloved fiancée will be hated as a wife. Why? Because as a wife she does not appear the same as she was imagined as a fiancée.
>
> However, God, who is loved when absent, does not diminish when he is present. No matter how much the human mind exaggerates God's goodness, it is still less than he is. Thus it is necessary that the possession of God find more than the mind could have imagined. So we will love him more when we see him, if we could have loved him even before we saw him. (1) (P)

Love seeks the good in the loved object. Thus even the misguided love of sin seeks a good. "You do not love sin, but merely love evilly that which you love, becoming ensnared in sin" (3). All creatures of God are good. It is only when we replace God with creatures that we sin.

Augustine contrasts delight in the world with delight in the Lord. "For he delights in the Lord when he destroys all delights in the world, and remains in the Lord in whom he rejoices and there remains in him a simple, perfect and immutable delight of heart" (9). After all, creatures are gifts of God who can give or take as he pleases. Thus when all of Job's possessions are taken away he can still rejoice in the Lord.

In Sermon 34, Augustine speaks on Psalm 149:1,2. "Sing the Lord a new song" (P). "A new man knows a new song. A song is a thing of joy, or better a thing of love. So whoever knows how to love a new life, knows how to love a new song" (1, 1).

> Charity is from God! There is no one who does not love. But it is asked what he loves. So we do not admonish not to love, but rather that we choose what we love. What or whom do we choose unless first we are chosen? Because we do not love unless first loved. Hear John the Apostle (Jn 13:23; 1 Jn 4:10). We love. How can we? Because he loved us first . . . He whom we love gave himself and he also gave that by which we love. What did he give us by which we love? Hear Paul! "The charity of God is diffused in our hearts." Whence does this love come? From us? No! Then whence? "Through the Holy Spirit who is given to us" (Rom 5:5). (1, 1)

Loving (*diligere*) is really choosing (*eligere*), both derivatives of *legere* (to choose or select). Augustine says that wrong loves are really wrong choices. When we choose God it is because he has chosen us first and given us the grace to choose him in return. When someone makes himself God, giving divine love to self or to a creature, trouble ensues.

A lascivious and impure person loves a beautiful woman. Bodily beauty moves him, but inside he seeks a return of love. For if he hears that she hates him, does not all his heat and desire for her lovely body cool? He recoils, turning offended from his heart's desire and begins to hate what he loved.
Has her shapely body changed? Is not everything still there that he had chosen? Everything is there all right! He loved in her what he saw and in his heart he wanted what he did not see. But if he finds out that he is loved in return, how his love grows stronger. She sees him, he sees her. No one sees love. Thus love is loved which is not seen. (2, 4)

Augustine's graphic description of unrequited love may well be experiential. Love is an invisible, intangible thing. Indeed, it is unseen, even as its divine author and object is invisible. When we love God, we possess him. "God you do not see. Love him and you possess him . . . God, in short, offers himself to us. He cries to us, 'Love me and you will have me, because you are not able to love me unless you have had me' " (3, 5).

What is the price of charity (*caritas*)? It is dear (*cara*), indeed! Though we can buy wheat with money, a farm with silver, pearls with gold, we must pay our very selves in order to buy charity.

If you want to have charity, seek yourself and find yourself. Why do you fear to give yourself, lest you be used up? Indeed, if you have not given yourself, you destroy yourself. Charity speaks through Wisdom, saying something to you. Are you not frightened at what it says: "Give yourself," . . . "Son, give me your heart" (Prov 23:26)? (4, 7)

The price of charity is self-gift. God gave himself to us so that we could give ourselves to God.
We should love God with our whole self and our neighbor as ourself.

Do you want to hear why you love yourself? You love yourself because you love God with your whole self. Do you think that God profits anything when you love him? Or because you love God he gains anything? And if you do not love him, does he lose anything?
When you love, you are the one who profits, for you will be there where you will not perish. But you will respond: When did I not

love myself? You did not love yourself when you did not love God who made you. But when you hated yourself, you thought that you were loving yourself. "Who loves iniquity, hates his own soul" (Ps 10:6). (5, 8)

Augustine's later works (411-30) are even more scriptural and less philosophical. Whether attacking the Donatists or commenting on the Psalms or on John or explaining the mysteries of the Trinity, scripture is the mainstay of his argument. He uses the Psalms, songs of love, as springboards for his sermons on love.

For example, commenting on Psalm 9:15, Augustine calls love the foot of the soul. When deformed, it is called lust but when healthy, it is named love or charity. When the foot of sinners is caught in a snare, it is most difficult to pull out.

In his second sermon on Psalm 31, Augustine speaks of active love.

Love itself cannot be idle. What but love is the active force, even for evil in man? Find me a love idle and unproductive! Crime, adultery, villainy, murder, excesses of all kinds, are they not the work of love? . . . Am I telling you "Love nothing?" Nonsense! Lazy, dead, detestable, wretched will you be if you love nothing. Love, but take care what it is that you love. The love of God and the love of one's neighbor are called charity. The love of earthly things, the love of this world, are termed passion. Bridle your passion, stir up your charity. (2, 5) (A)

Those in Christ's body are united in their love of him. So our love of Christ is not a jealous love. Not like a man craving to see a certain beautiful woman in the nude, but who does not want others to see her bare. No, the love of a Christian is not at all like this. For he wants others to love Christ as well. "Shame on those who love God in such a way as to begrudge him to others." People of the world are attached to an athlete or an actor and try to persuade others to support him.

Yet a Christian never raises his voice in church to invite others to join him in loving God's truth! Stir up this love in yourselves, then, brethren, and cry out to one another, saying, "O magnify the Lord with me." Let there be this glowing desire in you.

Why am I quoting and explaining these words to you? If you love God, carry along all those connected with you, and everybody in your house, and make them love God. If Christ's body, that is to say, the unity of the church, is the object of your love, urge them on to delight in it. Cry, "O magnify the Lord with me" (Ps 33:2).

The lover finds strength in the Holy Spirit.
For whatever thing is difficult in a commandment, is a light thing
to a lover. Nor on any other account is rightly understood the
saying "My burden is light" (Mt 11:30). But because he gives
the Holy Spirit whereby love is shed abroad in our hearts (Rom
5:5) in order that in love we may do freely that which he that
does in fear does slavishly. Nor is he a lover of what is right,
when he would prefer, if it were possible, that what is right should
not be commanded (Ps 68:16). (N)

All of our good works are really one work of love, for love is the
fulfilling of the law. "There is, therefore, one work, in which are all,
'Faith which works by love' " (Gal 5:6; Ps 90:17).

Love is the law of the city of God.
What is the city of God, but the holy church? For men who love
one another and who love God who dwells in them constitute a
city unto God. Because a city is held together by some law, their
very law is love. And that very love is God. For openly it is
written, "God is love" (1 Jn 4:8). He, therefore, who is full of
love is full of God. And many, full of love, constitute a city full
of God (Ps 99:4).

Augustine takes up this theme again in his *City of God.*

Trinity of Love

In his sermons on the Trinity, Augustine reaches a new psychological level of love talk. First of all, God is love. Secondly, we are made
to the image of God's self-love, so that our self-love must somehow
reflect God's love.

Justice is the basis of love, writes Augustine.
He, therefore, who loves men ought to love them either because
they are just or that they may be just. So ought he to love himself
also, either because he is just or that he may be just, for in this
way he loves his neighbor as himself without any danger. (8, 6)
(F)

As in some of his other works, Augustine draws a sharp distinction
between true love (*caritas*) and desire (*cupiditas*). "But this is true
love, that while holding fast to the truth, we may live justly. And,

therefore, we may despise everything mortal for the sake of the love of men whereby we wish them to love justly" (8, 7).

Scripture commands love of God and neighbor.
But he who loves God must logically do what God commanded, and loves him just as much as he does so. Therefore, he must also love his neighbor, since God has commanded this . . . But this also follows logically, for he who loves his neighbor must also love love itself above everything else. But "God is love and he who abides in love abides in God." Therefore, he must love God above everything else. (8, 7)

Let no one say "I do not know what I should love." Let him love his brother and he will love the same love, for he knows the love by which he loves more than the brother whom he loves. And so God can now become more known to him than his brother — actually more known because more present, more known because more within him, more known because more certain. Embrace love, God, and embrace God by love. (8, 8)

God is love, scripture says. But where is the triune nature of God in this? Augustine shows the threefold nature of love. We love love (God) and our brother or sister: lover, love and beloved. "If he loved him whom he sees by human sight with a spiritual love, he would see God, who is love itself, with that inner sight by which he can be seen."

Now love is of someone who loves, and something is loved with love. So then there are three: the lover, the beloved and love. What else is love, therefore, except a kind of life which binds or seeks to bind some two together, namely the lover and the beloved? (8, 10)

When the mind loves itself, it makes known two things, the mind and the love.

Yet mind and love are not two spirits, but one spirit; not two essences, but one essence. And still the two are one, the lover and the love, or, so to say, the beloved and love. These two are truly said to be related. The lover is referred to the love and the love to the lover, and love is of someone who loves. (9, 2)

But how is the Trinity reflected here?
Just as there are two things, the mind and its love, when it loves itself, so there are two things, the mind and its knowledge, when

it knows itself. Therefore, the mind itself, its love and knowledge are a kind of trinity. These three things are one and when they are perfect, they are equal. (9, 4)

If we love ourselves either more or less than we should, for example, if we deify ourselves, we sin.

Augustine continues:

In these three, when the mind knows itself and loves itself, the trinity remains: the mind, love and knowledge. And there is no confusion through any commingling, although each is a substance in itself, and all are mutually in all, whether each one is in each two, or each two in each one. Consequently, all are in all. (9, 5, 12)

This, then, is the trinity of the human soul: mind, love and knowledge, reflecting in highest manner the triune image of its Creator.

Another human triad which reflects the divine Trinity is the mind remembering, understanding and loving itself (14, 8).

Hence this trinity of the mind is not on that account the image of God because the mind remembers itself, understands itself and loves itself, but because it can also remember, understand and love him by whom it was made. And when it does so, it becomes wise. But if it does not, even though it remembers itself, knows itself and loves itself, it is foolish. Let it, then, remember its God, in whose image it has been made, and understand him and love him. (14, 12)

To forget God is sin. And what is more wretched than for us to be without him whom we cannot be without.

Though God is love, love is the special appropriation of the Holy Spirit.

When God, the Holy Spirit, therefore, who proceeds from God, has been given to man, he inflames him with the love for God and his neighbor, and he himself is love. For man does not have the means to love God, except from God himself (Rom 5:5). (15, 17)

The Spirit is especially called the Gift for no other reason except love. And if we do not have this love, even if we have all other gifts, we are nothing (1 Cor 13:1-3).

Furthermore, if among the gifts of God, none is greater than love, and there is no greater gift of God than the Holy Spirit, what is more logical than that he himself should be love, who is called both God and of God? And if the love whereby the Father loves the Son and the Son the Father reveals in an ineffable manner the union between both, what more fitting than that he who is the Spirit, common to both, should be properly called love? (15, 19)

So for Augustine God is a Trinity of love which is especially appropriated to the Holy Spirit. And we reflect the triune God especially when we remember, understand and love God.

Spiritual Love of the School of John

What better place to find a theology of love than the school of John (414-16).

Our love is determined by its object.
Those who love the world are called the world. By our loving we dwell with our hearts. But because of their loving the world, they deserved to be called after the name of that in which they dwelt . . . Those who do not love the world in the flesh still sojourn in the world, but in their hearts they dwell in heaven. (2, 11) (N)

Love of God and neighbor are interrelated.
He who commanded you this love in two precepts did not charge you to love your neighbor first, and then God, but first God and afterwards your neighbor. You, however, since you do not yet see God, earn to see him by loving your neighbor. By loving your neighbor, you purge your eye for seeing God (1 Jn 4:20).
Therefore, love your neighbor, look at the source of the love of your neighbor. There you will see God . . . Where does your way go, but to the Lord God whom we ought to love with the whole heart and with the whole soul and with the whole mind? For although we have not yet come to the Lord, we have our neighbor with us right now. (17, 8-9)

Our minds are drawn to God by love.
It is not enough to be drawn by the will. You are even drawn by delight. What is it to be drawn by delight? "Delight yourself in the Lord and he shall give you the desires of your heart" (Ps

37:4). There is a pleasure of the heart to which that bread of heaven is sweet.

Thus we are drawn to Christ when we delight in truth, blessedness, righteousness and life everlasting. "Give me a man that loves, and he feels what I say. Give me one that longs, one that hungers, one that is traveling in the wilderness and thirsting after the fountain of his eternal home. Give such and he knows what to say" (26, 4). This is the weight of love, which draws us to God.

The Holy Spirit is the personification of divine love. Why was the Spirit sent after the resurrection?

In order that our resurrection of love may be inflamed, and may part from the love of the world to run wholly toward God. For here we are born and die. Let us not love this world. Let us migrate hence by love, by love let us dwell above, by that love by which we love God. . .
If we live, if we believe in him who has risen again, he will give us, not that which men love here who love not God, or love the more the less they love him, but love this the less, the more they love him . . . Because such is what he promised to us who love him and grow with the charity of the Holy Spirit. (32, 9)

When the Holy Spirit came upon the early Christians, they became a community of love.

A considerable community was created in which all receiving the Holy Spirit, by whom spiritual love was kindled, were by their very love and fervor of spirit welded into one . . .

If by approaching God many souls by love become one soul and many hearts one heart, what of the very fountain of love in the Father and the Son? Is it not still more so here that the Trinity is one God? For thence of that Holy Spirit does love come to us, as the apostle says, "The love of God is shed abroad in our hearts by the Holy Spirit which is given to us" (Rom 5:5).
If, then the love of God, shed abroad in our hearts by the Holy Spirit which is given to us, makes many souls one soul and many hearts one heart, how much more are the Father, Son and Holy Spirit one God, one light and one beginning? (39, 5)

Christ has given us a new commandment to love each other as he has loved us. This is the love that renews us, makes us new heirs of the New Testament, singers of the new song. The twofold command-ment of love of God and neighbor does not contradict.

> For, on the one hand, he who loves God, cannot despise his command to love his neighbor. And, on the other hand, he who in a holy and spiritual way loves his neighbor, what does he love in him but God? That is the love distinguished from all mundane love, which the Lord specially characterized, when he added, "As I have loved you." For what was it but God that he loved in us? Not because we had him, but in order that we might have him, and that he may lead us on, as I said a little while ago, where God is all in all. (65, 1)

Likewise, when a physician loves the sick, he loves in them the health that he desires to recall. So we should love one another, hoping to have God in us. He loved us that we might love each other united in a body of which he is the head.

> Charity or love is the greatest and it fulfills the law.
> Although in charity, that is in love, are comprehended the two commandments, yet it is here declared to be the greatest only, and not the sole one . . . Love is the fullness of the law (Rom 15:10), and so where there is love what can be wanting? And where it is not, what is there that can possibly be profitable? The devil believes, but does not love. No one loves who does not believe.
> One may indeed hope for pardon who does not love, but he hopes in vain. But no one can despair who loves. Therefore, where there is love, there of necessity will be faith and hope. And where there is love of our neighbor, there also of necessity will be the love of God. For he that loves not God, how can he love his neighbor as himself, since he does not even love himself? (84, 3)

Few have this motive for loving each other, namely, that God may be all in all.
Peter made a threefold love commitment to Jesus, who asked him, " 'Do you love me?' 'Feed my sheep.' That is, 'If you love me, think not of feeding yourself, but feed my sheep as mine.' "

> Let us, then, love not ourselves, but him. And in feeding his sheep, let us be seeking the things which are his, not the things which are our own. For in some inexplicable way, I know not what, everyone who loves himself and not God, loves not himself,

and whoever loves God and not himself, he it is that loves himself. (123, 5)

Augustine also comments on the First Epistle of John, the love testament of the School of John.

> The deeds of men are only discerned by the root of charity. For many things may be done that have a good appearance, and yet proceed not from the root of charity, for thorns also have flowers. Some actions truly seem rough and savage, though they are done for discipline at the bidding of charity.
> Once and for all, then, a short precept is given you. Love, and do what you will, whether you hold your peace, through love hold your peace. Whether you cry out, through love cry out; whether you correct, through love correct; whether you spare, through love spare. Let the root of love be within, of this root can nothing spring but what is good. (7, 8)

> If any of you perhaps wish to keep charity, brethren, above all things do not imagine it to be an abject and sluggish thing; nor that charity is to be preserved by a sort of gentleness, nay not gentleness, but tameness and listlessness. . .
> Let charity be fervent to correct, to amend. But if there be good manners, let them delight you. If bad, let them be amended, let them be corrected. Love not in the man his error, but the man; for the man God made, the error man himself made. Love that which God made, love not that which man himself made. (7, 11)

> A father sometimes corrects his son fiercely. But, this is the fierceness of love, the fierceness of charity, a sort of fierceness without gall after the manner of the dove, not of the raven. Whence it came into my mind, my brothers, to tell you, that those violators of charity are they who have made the schism. As they hate charity itself, so they also hate the dove. (7, 11)

Brotherly and sisterly love is the theme of the Epistle of John, with less stress on the love of God and no mention of the love of enemies. Extend your love to them that are nearest. Yet do not call this an extending. For it is almost loving yourself, to love them that are close to you. Extend it to the unknown, who have done you no ill. Pass even them; reach on to love your enemies. This at least the Lord commands. Why has the apostle here said nothing about loving an enemy? (8, 4).

How should we love, *amare* (carnal love) or *deligere* (a higher love)? Not as a glutton loves his food and drink.

Whenever we love (*amamus*) in the way of food, to this end we love it that it may be consumed and we may be restored. Are men and women to be so loved as to be consumed? But there is a certain friendliness of well-wishing by which we desire at some time or other to do good to those whom we love. What if there be no good that we can do? The benevolence, the wishing well, of itself is sufficient for him who loves.

But what about those who are not in need? Can we still love them? "With a truer touch of love you love the happy man to whom there is no good office you can do. Purer will that love be and far more unalloyed." Love for the lowly tends to be patronizing, leading to pride. "Wish him to be your equal, that you both may be under the one Lord, on whom nothing can be bestowed" (8, 5).[1] John's school of love plays an important role in the later Augustine's theology of love, as the school of Plato did in his earlier days.

Charity, the Crown of the Virtues

Augustine discusses charity in his *Enchiridion* (421-22). Why is it called the crown of the virtues? "A man with right love also has right faith and hope. However, one who has no love, believes in vain even though what he believes may be true" (31) (A).

Man has four states: first, before the Law; second, under the Law; third, under grace; and fourth, full and perfect peace. In the third stage, "if God looks upon him, and he then believes that God helps him to carry out his commands and begins to be moved by the Spirit of God, then, with charity the dominant force in him, his desires run counter to his flesh" (31).

The whole Law depends on charity, for God is charity. Every commandment, therefore, has for its end charity, that is, it is charity that determines every commandment. But whatever is done either through fear of punishment or from some carnal motive so as not to be determined by that charity which the Holy Spirit diffuses in our hearts, is not done as it ought to be done, all appearances notwithstanding. (32)

So all the commandments, whether they be: thou shalt not commit adultery, kill, etc. "All these things are carried out in the right manner

---

1. See also *On Cathechizing* 4, 7.

when they are motivated by the love of God, and because of God, for our neighbor."

Love holds sway here and in the world to come. Thus we love God now through faith, then by sight. Here we love our neighbor through faith also, for we do not know what lies in his heart. But in the next world all will be revealed. "Who then can fathom how great love will be in the world to come, where there will be no passion for it to overcome or even restrain?"

City of Love

In his *City of God* (413-423) Augustine reviews some of his earlier love themes, namely, that our highest good is God and our love is a weight drawing us to God. The eternal law of love expresses this. Yet our egocentricity is still love's chief enemy.

Augustine's central thesis describes two cities, of God and man, based on two loves.

> What we see, then, is that two societies have issued from two kinds of love. Worldly society has flowered from a selfish love which dared to despise even God, whereas the communion of saints is rooted in a love of God that is ready to trample on self. In a word, this latter relies on the Lord, whereas the other boasts that it can get along by itself.
> The city of man seeks the praise of men, whereas the height of glory for the other is to hear God in the witness of conscience. The one lifts up its head in its own boasting. The other says to God, "You are my glory, you lift up my head" (Ps 3:4). (14, 28)[1]

In the city of the world the rulers and people are consumed by the lust for domination, whereas in the city of God all serve each other in charity. The one city loves its leaders as symbols of power, while the other loves God as its strength.

Love is the foundation stone of a city, writes Gilson.[2] "If we give the name 'city' to any group of men united by a common love for some object, we say that there are as many cities as there are loves." Those with earthly love (*cupiditas*) form an earthly city, while those with a heavenly love (*caritas*) form a heavenly metropolis. The two cities have coexisted since the beginning of the world. And in fact in

1. *The City of God*, tr., G. Walsh et al. (Garden City: Doubleday, 1962), 321.
2. E. Gilson, *The Christian Philosophy of Saint Augustine* 172.

each one's heart there are two loves, though we often tend more to one city than the other.

The people in a city are united by their common love. Moreover, most societies want to live in peace. But to have peace, order must be maintained, the harmony of a number of wills working for a common end. Augustine adds, "The peace of the heavenly city lies in a perfectly ordered and harmonious communion of those who find their joy in God, and in one another in God" (19, 13). Though the only city worthy of the name is the heavenly one, in the earthly life the two cities are intermingled.

The church is the kingdom of God (20, 9). But is it also the city of God? There are two kingdoms of God, one temporary and earthly, including saints and sinners, while the final reign is only for the elect. And this is the city of God.[1]

The two cities here below are contemporaneous and interwoven in each one of us, in the family, city and state. Can there ever be a perfect city of divine love on this earth? The history of monasticism has been a long-enduring attempt to reach this ideal with cities in the desert or on islands, etc. Augustine himself was drawn to this utopian life. But even here the city of man tended to creep in.[2]

In concluding our discussion of Augustine's theology and psychology of love, let us remark once again that although he started out Platonic, he ended up Pauline and Johannine. His theology of love was to influence generations of theologians and mystics, including Bernard, Aquinas and Luther.

In the following chapter we will see Augustine's theology of marriage which is the epitome of our supernatural love of our neighbor in whom we see God.

---

1. *Ibid.*, 333. See also Augustine's Commentary on Psalm 99, 4.
2. See J. Mohler, *The Heresy of Monasticism* (New York: Alba House, 1971), *passim.*

V.
THE MARRIAGE OF MALE AND FEMALE IS SOMETHING GOOD

(On the Good of Marriage, Chapter 3)

Ambrose: Heavenly Sacrament [1]

Ambrose, bishop of Milan and Augustine's mentor, helps lay the groundwork for his spiritual son's theology of marriage. Though he stresses the consent and progeny orientation of Roman matrimony, Ambrose also sees holy wedlock as a healing remedy for wounded human souls, following Judaeo-Christian traditions.[2]

Marriage is a divine gift to men and women, sanctified in a special way by Christ. So we should be especially careful not to destroy this sacred presence through divorce. For one who sins against marriage loses the grace of this heavenly sacrament (*On Abraham* 1, 7).

Ambrose, like most of his predecessors, follows Paul's theology of marriage, basing its sanctity on the union of Christ with his beloved spouse, the church. The Christian wife, like mother church, brings forth new members to be received and baptized.

We know God, as the watcher and guard of marriage, does not suffer the marriage bed of someone else to be defiled. And if anyone does this, we know that he sins against God, whose law he violates, whose grace he loses.

God's presence remains with the couple as long as they are at peace. However, mixed marriages can cause disharmony. For how can the nuptials be sanctified, if one spouse does not believe? (L 19). Yet Paul

---

1. This chapter first appeared in *Love, Marriage and the Family* (New York: Alba House, 1982); revised, 1988.
2. See W. Dooley, *Marriage According to St. Ambrose* (Washington: CUA Press, 1948).

says that the believing partner can sanctify her unbelieving mate (1 Cor 7:14).

Husband and wife have equal rights and duties, for neither is allowed intercourse with strangers. However, preserving mutual love and respect for the whole of married life is not easy. Affection, service, harmony and cheerfulness help preserve love. The husband should never lord it over his wife, for she is not his servant, but his spouse (L 63). But what if the husband has to go away on a long business trip! "The same bond of nature links together the rights of conjugal love between those who are far apart, as well as between those who are together. For they are both united by the yoke of the same blessing."[1] In Hebrew tradition the heavenly mother, the Shekhinah of Yahweh, who binds husband and wife, accompanies the husband when he is away on a trip.

As in the Roman and Pauline ideal, Ambrose stresses marital chastity, the man of one wife and the woman of one husband. He also teaches temperance especially in old age which is more suitable for governing than procreation (On Luke 1:43). Furthermore, Ambrose suggests moderation in matters of sex, for excesses can draw one away from the faith.

Since the purpose of marriage is the generation and education of children, abortion and child abuse are counterproductive, for even animals protect their own progeny. The parents' obligations are only beginning at the birth of their children, for they must feed, care for, clothe, house, give good example to and educate their youngsters, who, in their turn, should support their mothers and fathers in their old age.

Ambrose opposes easy Roman divorce. Although husband and wife may separate for adultery, they may not divorce, for this makes the children rootless, and the unborn suffer even more. Moreover, the divorced spouses are subject to grave temptations. How cruel it is for a husband to abandon the wife of his youth, when she gets old and wrinkled, for a young and pretty face and body.

Though Ambrose honors virginity in the Roman tradition, he notes that if there were no matrimony, there would be no virgins, since virgins are the fruit of marriage. Chastity is required of all Christians according to their different gifts: virgins, widows and spouses.

Augustine's Unequal Marriage

Augustine, educator, rhetor, philosopher and spiritual son of

---

1. *Hexaemeron* 5, 7.

Ambrose lived in an unequal marriage[1] for thirteen years during which he fathered a brilliant son, Adeodatus. Monica, Augustine's *mater familias,* felt that it would be in his best interest if he would leave his slave girl in order to wed the daughter of a wealthy patrician in an equal union (*matrimonium justum*).

When he was bishop of Hippo, Augustine looked back at his youthful wanderings and wrote them out in his *Confessions* to help others going through the same problems.[2] His insatiable sexual desires kept dragging him down. "They clouded over and darkened my soul so that I could not distinguish the calm light of chaste love from the fog of lust" (2, 2).

"There is a natural attraction in human bodies. For the sense of touch, what is suitable to it affords great pleasure." Each of the other senses delights in bodily indulgence as well. "I was tossed about and spilt out in my fornications. I flowed out and boiled over in them, but you kept silent." The Lord allowed Augustine to wallow in his impurities. "For you fashion sorrow into a lesson for us" (2, 2-4).

> In those years I had a companion, not one joined to me in what is named lawful wedlock, but one whom my wandering passion, empty of prudence, had picked up. But I had this one only and I was faithful to her bed. With her I learned first hand how great a distance lies between the restraint of a conjugal covenant, mutually made for the sake of begetting offspring, and the bargain of a lustful love, where a child is born against his will, although, once born, he forces himself upon our love. (4, 1)

However, Augustine's union with his peregrine was not unusual for the time, and later could be considered a marriage, unless stated to the contrary. "Even the Catholic Church was prepared to recognize it, provided that the couple remained faithful to one another" (S 312).

To Marry or Not

Alypius, Augustine's friend and fellow philosopher, tried to convince him not to marry so that he could devote his time to speculation. Augustine, too, feared the obligation of a permanent union. "For whatever conjugal dignity there is in raising children, it attracted neither of us, unless very lightly" (6, 12).

---

1. *Matrimonium injustum.*
2. *Confessions,* J. Ryan, tr. (Garden City: Doubleday, 1960).

Monica wanted her son Augustine baptized and settled into a good matrimony. However, the girl she had picked was two years below the legal age of consent. It was only with great reluctance that Augustine asked his faithful companion and mother of Adeodatus to leave. "This was a blow that crushed my heart to bleeding, for I loved her dearly" (6, 15). She returned sadly to Africa, ever loyal to her beloved Augustine, "vowing never to know man again."

Since two years was a long wait for his new bride, Augustine moved in with another girl. "By her my soul's disease would be fostered and brought safe, as it were, either unchanged, or in a more intense form, under the convoy of continual use into the kingdom of marriage."

However, fear of death and judgment jogged Augustine's conscience. Though blinded to interior beauty because of his attraction to bodily charms, yet he hears a voice calling out to him, "Run forward, I will bear you up" (6, 16).

In his *Soliloquies* at Cassiciacum (386-87) Augustine debates whether to marry or to continue his leisurely philosophical discussions with his companions. Would not a well-placed, fair, modest, obedient, intelligent wife be nice? But on the other hand, "If it is a part of a wise man's duty to devote himself to children, the man who takes a wife for this sole reason can seem to me to be worthy of admiration, not imitation" (1, 10) (F).

In the past Augustine had longed for a wife who would "in good repute bring me sensual satisfaction." Though he successfully spurns feminine embraces during his daytime reveries, at night, lying awake in his bed "you realized how differently from your claims those imagined caresses and their bitter sweetness excited you, far, far less than you were wont to do, but also far different from what you expected."

The hidden Physician pointed out to Augustine not only what he had escaped under his guidance, but also what remained to be healed. Augustine makes no claim to soundness "until I shall have looked upon that Beauty."

Adeodatus joins Augustine and Alypius in baptism by Ambrose in 387. "In that boy I owned nothing but the sin. That he was brought up by us in your discipline, to that, you and none other, inspired us. Your gifts I confess to you" (*Confessions* 9, 6). God took Adeodatus home to heaven shortly thereafter. Augustine would always remember him as a virtuous youth, the same age as his father in grace.

Pastoral Concern

As bishop Augustine defends the sanctity and indissolubility of marriage. For example, he challenges the Manicheans who downgraded the body, sex and marriage. God created all things good. So the battle is not between the evil body and the good soul, but rather the weak flesh confronts the Spirit of God within. Continence, far from despising sex, rather sublimates something good for something better.[1]

Augustine calls our tendency to sin concupiscence, dating back to the sin of Adam and Eve, and, similar to the Jewish *yetzer ha-ra,* which, though good, is prone to error especially in sexual matters.

In his *Commentary on the Sermon on the Mount* (393-96) (F) (Mt 5:27-28), Augustine notes that Jesus not only condemned adultery in deed, but also adultery of the heart, "which is the giving of such full consent that the aroused desire for it is not suppressed, but would be satisfied if the opportunity presented itself."

The three steps to sin: suggestion, pleasure and consent, parallel the garden story: the temptation by the serpent, the sin of Adam and Eve, and the expulsion from Eden. Moreover, the three degrees of sin: heart, deed and habit, reflect: death, the carrying out of the body and burial.

Jesus taught against divorce because it is the cause of adultery (Mt 5:31-32). When Moses ordered that a bill of divorce be written out, he wanted to moderate the husband's anger and delay the separation. Only for a grave reason such as fornication should a wife be put away. And he commands that all other annoyances be steadfastly borne for the sake of conjugal fidelity and chastity. Paul also teaches reconciliation.

What about the puzzling paradox of preferring Christ to our own family (Mt 10:34-37)? Since there is no marriage in the kingdom, temporal relationships should be seen as transitory. Can one love his wife as a human being, but abhor the shortness of their union? "The disciple of Christ must hate the things that are transitory in those persons whom he wishes to come with him to the things that endure. The more he loves those persons, so much the more must he hate those things."

A Christian can live in harmony with his wife in procreating union or in companionship as a brother. "At all events, he can live with her in such harmony that in her he loves the hope of eternal blessedness, even though he dislikes in her that which goes by the relationship of time." Perhaps here Augustine is facing the myth of growing old together. For there is an underlying fear of the finiteness of marriage, of widowhood and loneliness. Time is the inexorable enemy of love.

---

1. *On Continence.*

In fact, most extramarital liaisons are futile attempts to turn back the clock. However, if matrimony is seen in the light of eternity, anxiety will disappear.

Augustine opposed the use of sex outside of marriage (*Against Faustus* 22, 61) (N). According to the natural law

> conjugal intercourse should take place only for the procreation of children and after the celebration of marriage, so as to maintain the bond of peace. Therefore, the prostitution of women merely for the gratification of sinful passion is condemned by the divine and eternal law. To purchase the degradation of another, disgraces the purchaser.

Judah thought that he lay with a harlot. (Actually it was his daughter-in-law.) He was disgraced by his intercourse with a prostitute and she sinned by her desire to have children by Judah. "It certainly would have been better to have remained childless than to become a mother without marriage."

As we have seen,[1] Augustine speaks of two types of love, *uti* and *frui*, use and enjoyment. In marriage *uti* is preferable because by this love one uses his or her spouse to help on the way to heaven, and so does not make of the beloved an object of selfish pleasure (*frui*).

Once married the spouse does not always appear the same as before the ceremony. For example, he or she may have married for money (S 21). Augustine says that if a wife loves her husband's riches, she is not chaste. For "if she really loves her spouse, she will love him also in his nakedness and poverty" (S 157) (N). However, if she only wants his wealth, when he goes bankrupt, she flees. On the other hand, if she really loves him, she will show more affection and pity in his penury.

Husband and wife are instruments of each other's salvation in sickness or health, riches or destitution. For in matrimony two are saved as one.

The Good of Marriage

Marriage is good, writes Augustine against the Manicheans (*On the Good of Marriage*) (401) (F). God made the first natural tie of human society — man and wife. "They are joined to each other, side by side, who walk together and observe together where they are walking."

---

1. See chapter five; also Augustine, *On Christian Doctrine* 1, 12.

In our earthly life, "the marriage of male and female is something good." Moreover, the Lord confirmed this by forbidding divorce and joyously celebrating the marriage feast at Cana.

Furthermore, "this does not seem to me to be a good solely because of the procreation of children, but also because of the natural companionship between the sexes." Thus the marriage of old people is also good. For, when the ardor of youth wanes, "the order of charity still flourishes between husband and wife" (chapter 3).

Perhaps it might be a good idea occasionally to refrain from sexual intercourse early in married life so that, as the couple ages, "the chastity of souls rightly joined together continues the purer — the more proved and secure, if valued." Procreation tames lust. "For a kind of dignity prevails when as husband and wife, they unite in the marital act, they think of themselves as mother and father."

Husband and wife owe each other fidelity to the marriage debt, "even if they demand its payment somewhat intemperately and inconstantly" (4). All violations are adulterous, for marital fidelity should be valued even over bodily health. However, some men are so incontinent and inconsiderate, that they do not even spare their pregnant wives.

Married people owe each other not only the fidelity of sexual intercourse for the purpose of procreating children, but also the mutual service in a certain measure of sustaining each other's weakness, for the avoidance of illicit sex. (6)

Augustine sees marital intercourse solely for the satisfaction of personal lust as selfish and faulty. This would seem to imply the positive and deliberate exclusion of procreation from the act. Augustine lauds marital chastity. For the marriage pact is a kind of sacrament, not even nullified by separation. "The bond of fellowship between married couples is so strong that, though it is tied for the purpose of procreation, it is not loosed for the purpose of procreation." Moreover, this tight union is a symbol of something greater, so that they are wedded, even when they are apart (7).

Augustine, like the other Fathers, and the Romans, too, sees virginity as an ideal. However, it is far better to marry than to be tortured by passion.

Intercourse for generation belongs properly to matrimony, while outside it is more for passion than for reason (10). Even the immoderate use of sex in marriage is tolerable lest lust break out into something worse. But what if a husband wants to use his wife in a manner against nature? This is more shameful than if she allows him to go to another woman.

Augustine sees the crown of marriage as "the chastity of procreation and faithfulness in rendering the debt" (11). The bodies of husband and wife are temples of the Holy Spirit, and holy if they remain faithful to themselves and to the Lord. Paul adds that the believing wife sanctifies the body of her unbelieving husband.

When Paul reminds us that the virgin has more time to think of the Lord, he is not saying that the faithful and chaste wife is not trying to please the Lord, but rather that she is too busy with family problems. Augustine, like many of the Fathers, realizes the crushing burden of family responsibilities especially in the unsure times of the collapsing Roman Empire.

However, some married women go out of their way to make special time for the Lord, pleasing him in reverence and chastity with the "inner life of your heart, in the imperishableness of a quiet and gentle spirit, which is of great price in the sight of the Lord." For example, Sarah lived in peace and chastity (12).

When marriage is entered in the city of God, "from the first union of the two human beings matrimony bears a kind of sacred bond. So it can be dissolved in no way except by the death of one of the parties." Moreover, this bond remains intact even if one spouse is sterile (15).

Just as food is necessary for our own good health, so sex promotes the welfare of the race. Both are made attractive by pleasure. But just as the misuse of food, that is, through gluttony, can harm the body, so also the abuse of sex can be detrimental to the individual and society. What should be done for a poor couple who, through no fault of their own, cannot conceive progeny? Augustine responds that it is better to die childless than to seek offspring from an unlawful union.

Furthermore, just as good children of an adulterous marriage do not excuse it, so bad offspring from a good union do not condemn it. Marriage among all peoples is for procreation, "so that children might be born properly and decently."

In the Roman, Pauline and patristic ideal, Augustine praises the man of one wife. Why? If one has two wives, he loses "a certain standard, as it were, to the sacrament, necessary not for the reward of a good life, but for the seal of ecclesiastical ordination." While the single marriage of clerics signifies the union of Christ with his church, the one wedlock of the laity reflects the unity of all under God in the heavenly city.

Just as apostasy from the one true God is adultery, so "in the marriage of our women, the sanctity of the sacrament is more important than the fecundity of the womb" (18). A marriage is good insofar as the couple "fear God more chastely and more faithfully, especially if they also nourish spiritually the child whom they desire carnally" (19).

Threefold Good

The good of marriage among all peoples "is in the cause of generation and in the fidelity of chastity." For the people of God the good of marriage also includes the sanctity of the sacrament. So Christian marriage contains a threefold good: *proles* (child), *fides* (fidelity) and *sacramentum* (sacrament), with all three elements inseparable. So there are not three individual goods of marriage, but rather one threefold good. Thus it is wrong to leave a spouse in order to beget progeny (24).

In his *Literal Commentary on Genesis* (9, 7-12) (P), Augustine changes the order of the threefold good to: fidelity, child and sacrament.

In fidelity one is careful not to lie with another outside the marriage bond. In the child, that it be lovingly received, kindly nourished and religiously educated. In the sacrament, however, that the union never be split, and the disowned one not be vowed to another for the purpose of childbearing. This is the rule of nature by which either the fecundity of nature is honored, or the depravity of incontinence is controlled.

Just as a priest's ordination for the people is still valid even though he has no congregation, or if he is removed from the ministry, so the marital bond still holds, even if the union is childless.

Augustine argues against many traditions, including some in his native Africa, which hold that childbearing is necessary for the validity of marriage, or which at least allow the taking of concubines in order to ensure offspring. He reflects the church's position in defending the rights of sterile women from dismissal in a patriarchal society. This is unjust because male sterility is overlooked.

Jesus Honors Marriage at Cana

Commenting on the Cana story (Jn 2:1-11), Augustine remarks,[1] "What wonder if he came to that house to a marriage, having come into this world to a marriage?" For if he did not come into this world to a marriage, he does not have here his bride, the church (2 Cor 11:3). "He gave his own blood for her, whom, rising again, he was to have, whom he had already united himself to in the virgin's womb."

---

1. *Commentary on John*, tr. 8, 4-5.

The Word of God is the bridegroom, while his human flesh is his bride. Together they are one, Son of God and Son of Man. "The womb of the Virgin, in which he became the head of the church, was his bridal chamber." And he came forth happy as a new bridegroom from his nuptial bedroom.

Why did Jesus seem to treat his mother with contempt at Cana? "Surely he to whose marriage he had come was taking a wife with the view of having children," who he hoped would, in turn, honor him as their father. Was the bridegroom shocked at Jesus' words to his mother, "What have you to do with me?" Later Augustine explains that this involves the mystery of the Incarnation, namely, the expected miracle pertains to his divinity, whereas Mary is the mother of his humanity. But still a mystery!

Cana was seen by early Christians as the model of the Christian marriage, blessed by the presence of Jesus, the divine bridegroom, in the company of his virgin spouse, the church, modelled on his virgin mother. We will see more of this in later chapters.

Marriage and Virginity

There was much disputation about which is better — marriage or virginity — at the time of Augustine. Augustine, Jerome and others argued for the priority of virginity based on the theology of the virginal mother and the virginal church.

Augustine comments that both married women and virgins consecrated to God by holiness and charity "are spiritually the mother of Christ because they do the will of his Father."[1] Married women give birth to Adams who soon become members of Christ through baptism.

When these good Christian mothers unite with their husbands in order to have progeny, they have no other concern for them but gaining them for Christ. And so they have them baptized as soon as possible through the motherhood of the church. "Inasmuch as she (the church) is spiritually the mother of Christ's members, she is also spiritually his virgin."

In this holy birth of baptism the mothers also cooperate who have brought forth non-Christians in the body that these may become what they could not bring forth in the body. Yet they cooperate through this in which they are also both virgins and

---

1. *Holy Virginity*, cc. 6-13.

mothers of Christ, namely, in faith which works through charity (Gal 5:6).

Which is better, a married woman or a virgin? (c. 11). A married woman is more blessed than a virgin who intends to marry, because the married woman already has what the virgin wants. The married woman tries to please one man, while the virgin wants to keep many happy. Though married women generate virgins, they do not give birth to consecrated virgins, whose mother is the church, for the consecrated virgin is the spouse of Christ (c. 12).

Let spouses have their blessing, not because they beget children, but because they beget them honorably and lawfully and chastely and for society and bring up their offspring rightly, wholesomely and with perseverance; because they keep conjugal fidelity with each other and because they do not desecrate the sacrament of matrimony.

The devoted consecrated virgin is angelic and a foretaste of heaven, for there is no marriage in heaven (Mt 22:35). "Let all carnal fecundity and conjugal chastity bow to this." Augustine prefers this motive for vowed virginity rather than the avoidance of the toil and burden of married life.

Adulterous Marriages

When Pollentius asks Augustine to clarify the common problem of divorce and remarriage, he responds in his work on *Adulterous Marriages* (419) (F) that the indissolubility of matrimony is based on its sacramentality.

Moreover, just as marriage heals errant human sexuality, so divorce prompts libido toward adultery. Even if a wife leaves her husband to pursue the continent calling of religious life, she still may be the unwitting cause of her spouse's sexual wanderings. So separation should never be attempted without the mutual consent of husband and wife (4).

But what if one spouse is acting immorally? The innocent mate may separate, but not remarry. Furthermore, it is wrong to separate if the other partner has not sinned. However, Augustine feels that adultery is less serious if one's unfaithful wife has been put away. But she remains his wife, even though separated. For husband and wife are bound to each other for life, and adultery is not death. "The woman begins to be the wife of no later husband, unless she has ceased to be the wife of the former one" (2, 4).

Augustine rejects the double standard common in patriarchal society, namely, punishing the erring wife, while looking the other way at her husband's antics. Since the husband should be an example of virtue for his wife, he should be punished more severely for adultery (2, 8). Thus Emperor Antoninus "did not allow a husband whose conduct did not furnish an example of chastity to accuse his wife of the crime of adultery." How much more should this be observed in the holy city of God? (2, 8). Since the marriage bond is valid till death, it renders any subsequent nuptials adulterous. However, it is a worse sin to divorce and remarry for a lesser cause than fornication (2, 9).

Christ's law displeases the incontinent who want to divorce a quarrelsome and domineering spouse. "It is this weakness, namely, incontinence, that the apostle wished to remedy by the sanctity of marriage" (2, 12).

Augustine, reflecting the Roman and Judaeo-Christian traditions, calls procreation the primary end of marriage. So it is shameful and unlawful "whenever the conception of offspring is avoided."

Moreover, a husband should remain continent even if his wife is an adulteress or is ill. Furthermore, he should never be vengeful against his erring spouse. "In the knowledge that they are not without sin, they forgive, in order that they may be granted forgiveness. Likewise, kindness and love will not be withheld from them" (2, 14).

In the last of his *Diverse Questions*[1] Augustine notes that Jesus said no divorce except for fornication (Mt 5:32). Though divorce is allowed in the case of pagan marriages, a Christian should not divorce an unbelieving spouse who wants to stay in the marriage (1 Cor 7:18).

In the case of fornication Christ was speaking to Christian spouses. "Hence if both are believers, then neither one is permitted to leave the other, except for reason of fornication." Christ tells the Christian wife not to leave her husband. "But if she does leave him, let her remain unmarried or be reconciled to him" (1 Cor 7:10-11). Moreover, even if she leaves because of his fornication, she still cannot remarry.

"But if she does not remain continent (she ought) to be reconciled to her husband, either after he has been straightened out, or when she can at least put up with him, rather than marry another."

When Paul says a husband should not divorce his wife, he negates the double standard under Hebrew law, "declaring in brief the same pattern for the man which he was prescribing for the woman" (1 Cor 7:11).

Paul in general quotes the Lord in his theology of marriage. But

---

1. *Eighty-Three Diverse Questions*.

on his own he says the believer should remain with an unbelieving spouse who wants to stay in the marriage (1 Cor 7:12-13).

We are bound under the law as long as we live. So the wife is one with her husband while he is living. Then she is free to marry whom she wants. "While her husband is living, she is called an adulteress, if she is with another man." But if her spouse is dead, she is free (Rom 7:2-3).

Marriage and Concupiscence

Husbands should take the lead in chastity. For many go on long business trips and expect their wives to remain chaste at home. Some men tend to confuse the male image with the license to sin. Moreover, Christian clerics and virgins should give good example by their chaste lives.

Augustine notes in his *Marriage and Concupiscence* (419-20) (P) that true chastity is a gift of God, inspired by faith (1, 3). However, the generative act of matrimony can be misused if it is only pursued for selfish pleasure (1, 4). Husband and wife should take special care not to defraud each other. Christian marriage is not only aimed at generation, but also at regeneration, in which the children are reborn as sons of God, transforming human members into the members of the body of Christ.

The natural shame connected with carnal pleasure does not condemn marriage. For Adam and Eve, whose union was blessed by God, were innocent in their nudity. They felt no unruly motions in their strong young bare bodies, "because since nothing preceded which was illicit, nothing followed which was shameful" (1, 5). However, when they disobeyed God, they blushed and grabbed some fig leaves to cover their privates. Yet the inclination toward pleasure does not detract from the good of marriage.

Marriage is indissoluble, and in this, secular law differs from the gospels. Not only fertility, whose fruit is the child, or chastity, whose link is fidelity, but also a certain sacrament of marriage is recommended to the faithful (L 5).

The responsibility of matrimony (legal relationship and rights) is the inseparable union till death, except in cases of fornication (Mt 5:32). This close bond is guarded by Christ and his church. The sacrament of marriage is observed in the city of God, the church of Christ, whose faithful married couples are the active limbs of his body.

There remains between the couple a living link which neither separation nor union can take away. Moreover, even when fidelity is lost, the sacrament of fidelity is not (1, 10). The holy family of Nazareth is a model of the threefold good of marriage.

Though intemperance among married couples may be tolerated, Augustine feels that the use of matrimony solely for selfish delight does not avoid some guilt. However, because of the good of marriage, it is slight. Moreover, he believes that those who use contraceptives are not true spouses. For example, some use sterilizing drugs, abort their fetuses or even expose the living infants (1, 14-16).

Once again he praises the threefold nuptial good: the child born for rebirth; fidelity to a spouse who is a member of Christ's body; and a sacrament which even adultery cannot destroy. This sacrament, which is great between Christ and his church, is mirrored in the human union.

In his Easter sermon to new converts, Augustine encourages them toward conjugal chastity. "You who have wives, do not admit any other interest. To you who do not have wives and want to marry, keep yourselves inviolate for your wives, as you desire to find them inviolate" (S 244).

Fear adultery as you would fear eternal death. Do you have a wife? "Any woman other than your wife who cohabits with you is a harlot."

"On the contrary, your wife is faithful to you. For she knows no other except you alone and does not contemplate knowing another. Since she is chaste, why do you fornicate? If she loves you alone, why do you love two women?"

But you may say, "I do not want to go to someone else's wife or to a prostitute, just to my own servant concubine. Should not the privacy of my own home be respected?" Augustine responds, "Those who act thus go to hell!!!" Do not wait until tomorrow to reform, saying over and over, "tomorrow, tomorrow" (*cras, cras*), like a crow. Augustine begs his newly baptized not to imitate those whom he has just described.

Augustine further discusses conjugal chastity in his *Trinity*.[1] "Conjugal chastity can make good use of carnal concupiscence which is strong in our genitals." Yet we still feel involuntary motions which were not felt by our first parents in the Garden of Eden; or if they were present, were under full control of the will.

Now we feel it to be such that it fights against the law of the mind and arouses desires for intercourse, even if there is no intention of begetting children. If we yield, then our lust is satisfied through sin. If we do not yield, then our carnal motions are restrained by withholding consent.

1. *The Trinity* 13, 18.

Marriage, Image of the Trinity

In a sense, the threefold good of matrimony mirrors the divine image. For example, procreation imitates the creativity of the Father. Fidelity reflects Christ's loyalty to his spouse, the church. And the sacrament points the way to the Holy Spirit who sanctifies the union, cementing its indissolubility.

Augustine considers intercourse for pure pleasure, excluding altogether the generative aspect, as a slight deviation in marriage. This is probably because of the selfishness of the act, excluding any reference to God, the regeneration of the Mystical Body of Christ or salvation, *frui* taking precedence over *uti*. But certainly this is a lesser fault than enjoying sexually one who is not his wife.

Marital affection mirrors the Divine Triad of Lover, Beloved and Love. In wedded bliss God is the Love between the spouses. "If he loved him (her) whom he sees by human sight, with a spiritual love, he would see God, who is love itself with that inner sight by which he can be seen."[1]

Since God is love, there cannot be true, lasting affection in marriage without him. Like God, the Christian marriage is creative, faithful and holy. So it cannot tolerate the frustrating threesome of contraception, adultery and desecration. Christian marriage is indissoluble because God, who is love, is at its core.

Marriage in the City of God [2]

God commanded Adam and Eve in the garden to increase and multiply and fill the earth (Gn 1:28). While there was no lust in Eden, after the fall, our first parents covered up their privates in shame.

God's blessing on their marriage with the command to increase their progeny and fill up the earth was given before the fall. However, his benediction remained even after they had sinned, because the begetting of children "is a part of the glory of marriage," and has nothing to do with the penalty for sin.

According to God's instruction and blessing, he gave to matrimony its mission, when he instituted it in the beginning (14, 22). This is why he made the bodies of male and female different. "And it was precisely on the conjugal duty itself that God's blessing fell." Male and

1. *Ibid.,* 8, 8.
2. *City of God* 14, 21.

female were made to increase and multiply and fill the earth by becoming mothers and fathers.

Jesus said that from the beginning God made them male and female. And that is why one leaves his father and mother, cleaves to his wife and the two become one flesh. So what God has joined no one should separate (Mt 19:3-6). Augustine remarks that these words obviously refer to the bond of matrimony by which a man and a woman are bound to each other. They are not to be taken in a spiritual or metaphorical sense.

So male and female were created in the beginning as they are now. The two are called one either because of the unity of marriage, or because Eve was taken from the side of Adam.

Paul refers to the matrimony of Adam and Eve as the ideal which was instituted by God from the beginning. So husbands should honor their wives (Eph 5:25).

Moreover, the generation of the saints to populate the city of the blessed would have taken place even if no one had sinned. This would be the same as the number of saints, past, present and future, "so long as there are parents and babies among the children of the world." In the Garden of Eden there would have been marriages worthy of that blessed place and lovely babies created without lust (14, 23).

Here we can control our other members, so why not our reproductive organs as well? Lust defies the soul, making the organs shameful. For the soul's self conquest to be perfect it needs to subdue the passions. Even partial control is better than none. Surely the will can restrain other bodily members which contribute to the "lust which excites the will." Thus passion remains, although its power is diminished.

Without the fall men and women in paradise would have been free from those "moral stresses and strains caused by the tensions between reason and passion." Moreover, without the fall, there would be no embarrassment in talking about sex without fear of offending pious ears. We could talk about the most intimate details without raunchy words or shameful body parts. Augustine follows the lead of Paul in his frank discussions of sexual matters (Rom 1:26).

In the Garden of Eden "family affection was ensured by the purity of love. For body and mind worked in perfect accord; and there was an effortless observance of the law of God." Since all the bodily members were submissive to the mind, men and women could conceive in serenity without lust (14, 26).

As we have seen, the first marriage was between Adam and Eve. Further unions took place among their progeny, with the men taking their sisters as their wives. Anthropologists tell us that most early marriages were between close relatives simply because of the inability to travel far from the home tribe (15, 16).

But the superior human law is love acting through harmony binding ourselves by the ties of social relationships, monogamous and widely distributed, "so that the common social life of the greatest number may best be fostered."

Adam was both father and father-in-law, while Eve was both mother and mother-in-law, as their sons and daughters married. But as the population increased there was a wider choice of spouses and they were bound by the law of love to do so.

"It is the right of love to have itself diffused, so that one love may hold together as many persons as possible." "The love which holds kindred together—embraces a greater number of people over a far wider area." This law of love is observed even by pagans.

Custom has great power in controlling human passions, keeping concupiscence in bounds, for example, by forbidding the marriage of first cousins. Augustine notes that this custom is morally sound. For it is "socially right to multiply and distribute relationships of love," rather than enclosed unions where one person has more than one relationship with another, that is, the double embarrassment of consanguineous lust.

The union of male and female is the seedbed from which a city grows. While the earthly city needs human generation, the city of heaven seeks spiritual rebirth.

Moreover, marital chastity is a requirement for the city of God. For a Christian who has a harlot in his heart and becomes one body with her, no longer builds on the firm foundation of Christ. On the other hand, "If anyone loves his wife and loves her 'according to Christ' he continues without any doubt to have Christ as his foundation" (21, 26).

However, even if he loves his wife "according to the world" with an exclusively carnal desire or with the diseased passions of the pagans, who do not know God, his marriage is legitimate as Christ and Paul teach. "Even such a man can have Christ for his foundation so long as he does not allow anything in his love and pleasure to come before Christ." Though he may build up his marriage with wood and straw, Christ is still his fundament. And he will be saved by the fire which destroys his flimsy house but saves him in the process.

"The pleasures of passionate love on earth are made legitimate by reason of the marital union, yet they do not escape such burning flames of tribulation as widowhood or other woes that take away wedded bliss."

So if we build our house of straw or wood, it will not last. And he suffers the loss of a loved one, the more she brought him joy and pleasure. Yet because of his foundation in Christ he will be saved through this burning fire of privation. For in the last analysis (that is, in persecution) he would choose Christ.

But what if we put our human loves above our love of Christ? (21, 26). Augustine is not only talking about sexual intercourse, but rather men "whose loves, though free from such indulgences, are so purely human that they are preferred to the love of Christ." These do not have Christ as the foundation of their marriages. Jesus warned that we should not chose our love of mother or father, husband or wife over our love for him (Mt 10:37).

Yet if we love our human relatives to the fullest extent possible and yet keep the first place in our hearts for Christ and even give up our human loves for love of Christ, we will be saved by fire, namely, the burning pain by which we give up even our friends for Christ's sake.

We should love our father or mother, husband or wife, son or daughter as Christ wants us to love them, that is, "to lead them to the kingdom of Christ's faith and love, or loving them because they are already one with Christ and a member of his body."

This love has Christ for its foundation, upon which we build our house of gold, silver and gems. For how can we love more than Christ those who are loved on account of Christ?

Conclusion

Augustine is a noted theologian of concupiscence, love and marriage. And since he had lived with a common-law wife for many years, he can speak from experience. As bishop of Hippo, Augustine's pastoral concern comes to the fore. Condemning the Manicheans who looked down on marriage, Augustine stresses, rather, its threefold good.

Upon the permanent sacramentality of matrimony Augustine bases its indissolubility, opposing the Roman policy of easy divorce. Furthermore, he places more responsibility on the husband to give good example to his wife and family.

Augustine accepts the child-orientation of Rome, Israel, Christianity and other cultures as well. It is wrong to frustrate this end, although fidelity takes precedence over progeny. Like Paul, Augustine reflects the Jewish *yetzer ha-ra* in his doctrine of concupiscence. However, since marriage is good, libido may be used well therein.

Although Augustine praises virginity, he also tells the virgin not to lord it over the God-fearing housewife. Virginity and marriage support each other. Though Christian families generate virgins, consecrated virginity, which imitates the church, the virgin spouse of Christ, is a gift of God. Although his saintly mother Monica encouraged Augustine to baptism and to marry well, he was ultimately drawn more to the monastic way. In the following chapter we will see why.

VI.

HOW GOOD AND PLEASANT IT IS WHEN BROTHERS DWELL IN UNITY

(On Psalm 133)

Augustine the Monk [1]

Christian monasticism grew strong during the fourth and fifth centuries under the influence of the gospels, Coptic and perhaps Hindu traditions. Christian ascetics or ascetics-to-be toured the monasteries and anchorites of Egypt and the Holy Places. Those who could not afford to travel devoured Egyptian monastic literature such as the *Life of Antony, Pachomius' Rules,* etc. Augustine, called the father of African monasticism, never visited Egypt, but was inspired by the *Life of Antony* and the pious monks of Milan and Rome. Moreover, he was quite familiar with the ascetical practices of northern Africa, some good, some questionable.

As early as the second century we find Montanist ascetics in Carthage. Living at home, rather than in community, the veiled virgins were honored with special places in the liturgy. By the time of Augustine, African monasticism was still in its primitive stages with itinerant monks moving from place to place with their repulsive dirty clothes and long straggly hair. Often trouble-makers, the monk-like Donatist circumcellions hung around the martyrs' shrines, begging, selling relics, attacking the Catholics and, in general, defying civil authorities.

While living in Milan, Augustine's friend Alypius tried to persuade him away from the attractions of married life into the leisurely life of a philosopher. But Augustine replied that many married men were also able to pursue a way of wisdom. Besides, he felt that he could never tolerate a life of celibacy.

---

1. This and the following chapter first appeared in *The Heresy of Monasticism* (New York: Alba House, 1971).

80

Yet the desire for a common life continued to grow among Augustine and his companions.

> Many of us who were friends, detesting the tumultuous annoyances of human life, had by now, through thinking of the matter and joint discussion, almost decided to live in a quiet way removed from the crowds. To secure this peaceful life, we planned to put together whatever possessions we had and set up one household out of all, so that as a result of true friendship, nothing would belong to one person rather than to another. Instead, one fund would be made of all our possessions, and the whole thing would belong to each person singly, and everything to all. (*Confessions* 6, 14) (F)

This was the prototype of the strict poverty of Augustine's religious community at Hippo. There were ten men in Augustine's Milan society, some of whom were wealthy, for example, Romanianus. Two managers were chosen to take care of all temporalities, holding office for one year, so that the others would be free for the leisurely life of philosophers, like their Greek and Roman predecessors. However, Augustine and his friends soon abandoned their utopian dreams when it occurred to them that their girl friends (*mulierculae*) would never tolerate their bachelorhood.

One day later on when Ponticianus, a Roman court officer, visited Augustine, he was impressed by a copy of Paul's epistles lying on a table. When Augustine explained that he regularly read the scriptures, Ponticianus told him the story of Antony the Egyptian hermit who was making such an impact on the West especially since his biographer Athanasius' exile in Rome and Trier. Antony's humble life, miracles, teaching and asceticism excited Augustine and Alypius and proved to be a turning point in their lives.

When he saw that he had sparked their interest, Ponticianus told them about the monks living in deserts or near cities. Actually there was a monastery just outside the gates of Milan, although Augustine and his friends were not aware of it.

Next Ponticianus told them of two of his fellow officers who, while wandering through a garden in Trier, came upon a house of the Lord's poor brethren in which they found a copy of Athanasius' *Life of Antony*. These Trier ascetics may have dated from Athanasius' visit there in 336. Leafing through Antony's *Life*, one of the officers suddenly felt the call to be a monk. Turning to his companion, he cried:

> Tell me, I beg you, what goal do we hope to achieve with all these efforts of ours? What are we looking for? What reason do

we have for engaging in public service? Could our aspiration at the court be anything greater than to become "Friends of Caesar?" Through how many dangers must one go to reach a greater danger? And when will one reach it? Now, if I wish, I can be a friend of God immediately. (*Confessions* 8, 6)

One could see that he was going through the pains of rebirth, turning away, stripping off his old worldly life and converting to the monastic way. "I have now broken away from our former hopes and have determined to serve God. From this very hour and in this very place I make my start. If it is too much for you to imitate me, do not oppose me." The two companions joined together in building a tower, breaking off their engagements with their fiancées who, in turn, dedicated themselves as virgins to Christ.

As Ponticianus related his story, Augustine began to look into his own life.

You, indeed, O Lord, did twist me back on myself, while his words were being spoken, taking me away from behind my back, where I had placed myself, and you set me right in front of my own face so that I might see how ugly I was, how deformed and vile, how defiled and covered with sores. I saw and was filled with horror, yet there was no place to flee from myself. If I attempted to turn my gaze away from myself, he kept on telling his story, and you again placed me before myself, thrusting me up before my eyes, so that I would discover my iniquity and detest it. I recognized it, but pretended not to. I thrust it from my sight and out of my mind. (*Confessions* 8, 7)

The more Augustine admired these men who had given themselves to Christ, the more he hated himself, for he had always been searching for the truth. Even in his Manichean days he had asked for the gift of continence, "but not yet." He excused his delay in leaving off worldly pleasures because he had not yet found anything certain on which to hang his hopes. Even now, although attracted to the monastic way, his old loves held him back.

Walking one day in the garden of his host, Augustine heard a child shouting, "*Tolle, lege*" (take and read). At first he thought it was a children's game. But then he remembered how Antony had been inspired by a gospel reading: "Go, sell whatever you have and give to the poor. You shall have your treasure in heaven. Come, follow me" (Mt 19:21) (*Confessions* 8, 12). Punning to Alypius, Augustine snatched up a volume of Paul which he had left on a table. Opening it, he spotted a passage from Romans (13:13-14): "Let us conduct ourselves becomingly as in the day, not in reveling and drunkenness, not in debauchery and licentiousness, not in quarreling and jealousy, but put on the Lord Jesus Christ, and make no provision for the flesh to gratify its desires." Instantly Augustine felt a peace flow over him. As the divine light flooded his heart, all dark shadows of doubt fled (8, 12). Full of joy, Augustine told his happy conversion first to Alypius and then to Monica.

The mystery of a vocation is often culminated in a dramatic moment. However, its seeds are usually long planted. Many prayers, sermons, the example of Monica, Ambrose, Victorinus, Ponticianus, Antony and others had plowed, planted and watered. But it was in the reading of Paul's Epistle to the Romans that God gave the increase.

During the first week of August, 386, Augustine determined to give up his profession as a rhetor to devote his life to philosophy. Since he had been under a strain due to a heavy teaching load and his own personal identity crisis, Augustine welcomed the use of his friend Verecundus' country place at Cassiciacum for rest and study, spending the fall and early winter there with his mother Monica, his elder brother Navigius, his son Adeodatus, some cousins, his friends Alypius and Evodius and two young boys sent to him for instruction. Here they pursued in a family way the philosophical life they had planned earlier. And Augustine began writing his dialogues: *Against the Academics, On the Happy Life, On Order,* and the *Soliloquies.*

These scholastic days Augustine calls "*Christianae vitae otium* (Christian leisure)" (*Retractations* 1, 1), which was to be his way of life until his ordination in 391. And even when bishop, Augustine continued to follow the communal contemplative way at Hippo. Although his life at Cassiciacum was not yet monasticism, it was a foreshadowing. The idea of monks as Christian philosophers was not foreign to Basil, Evagrius nor later to Dardanus, a retired prefect who would turn his village in the lower Alps into a theopolis of Christian wisdom.

While enjoying his philosophical leisure, Augustine planned that after a good marriage and perhaps a term as a civil magistrate, he might retire with honor and privilege to just such a country villa for the rest of his life.

But he soon abandoned all such plans, while continuing his soul-searching as his *Soliloquies* testify. Meditating and reading scriptures, he formally resigned his post as civil rhetorician in Milan and along with Alypius and Adeodatus presented himself to Ambrose for baptism during the Easter vigil of 387. Rising naked as a new-born baby from the cold baptismal waters, Augustine felt entirely renewed, his past life of sin dead and gone. Drawn to the monastic way, he visited Ambrose's monastery outside the city gates.

Joined by Evodius, Augustine's group resembled a monastic community more than the philosopher's study club at Cassiciacum. They intended to return as soon as possible to Thagaste where they would continue their semi-monastic life in Augustine's family home.

During a delay at Ostia, Monica died, having seen her wishes fulfilled in her son's conversion. Grieving, Augustine went to Rome where he visited some of the local monasteries and continued his writings. Though by nature Augustine was a contemplative and a writer, by force he was to become also an ecclesiastical administrator.

While in Rome, he became angry with the Manicheans who arrogantly considered themselves superior to ordinary Christians because of their continence and abstinence by which the elect could approach the uncontaminated light.

In comparing Catholic and Manichean morals (388),[1] Augustine employs the customary argument, namely, contrasting the saintly Christian way of life with the corrupt morals of the Manicheans. Although he praises the frugal fathers of the desert, Augustine does not tarry here since some accuse them of abandoning their neighbor, while others feel that they have gone too far in their ascetical rigors. Augustine goes on to praise the cenobites who are his inspiration.

Who can but admire and commend those who, slighting and discarding the pleasures of this world, living together in a most chaste and holy society, unite in passing their time in prayers, in readings, in discussions, without any swelling of pride, or noise of contention, or sullenness or envy; but quiet, modest and peaceful, their life is one of perfect harmony and devotion to God, an offering most acceptable to him from whom the power to do these things is obtained? No one possesses anything of his own, no one is a burden to another. They work with their hands in such occupations as may feed their bodies without distracting their minds from God. (31)

They give the products of their work to the deans, who supply the monks whatever they need for their sustenance. So without temporal worries, they are free to contemplate. The abbot, saintly and learned, rules with humility, instructing the monks daily before the main meal. Eating frugally, they avoid wine and meat which tickle the passions. Moreover, they distribute any excess to the poor.

---

1. *The Morals of the Catholic Church and the Morals of the Manicheans* (388) (N).

There are also Christian nuns who serve God assiduously and chastely, living apart and removed as far as propriety demands from the men, to whom they are united only in pious affection and in imitation of virtue. No young men are allowed access to them, nor even old men, however respectable and approved, except to the porch to furnish necessary supplies. (32)

The nuns weave cloth which they give to the men in exchange for food.

Although Augustine claims that he is not eulogizing the Christian ascetics, he comes very close to this. Later he will be more realistic in his *On the Work of the Monks* (400) and in Sermons 355 and 356, where he chastises monastic abuses.

Later in his *Morals* Augustine describes other Christian ascetics who live in urban lodging houses, presided over by a presbyter, eminent in virtue and learning, charity, holy, free, ruling in a Pauline manner. Self-supporting, they fast rigorously, sometimes going three days without food or drink. There are also pious women, widows and virgins, spinning and weaving, governed by a prudent and experienced woman. Often a male ascetic such as Jerome or Pelagius served as chaplain.

The law of charity governs these Christian ascetics. There is charity in their choice of diet, charity in their speech, charity in their dress, charity in their looks. Charity is the point where they meet, and the plan in which they act. To transgress against charity is thought criminal, like transgressing against God. Whatever opposes this is attacked and expelled; whatever injures it is not allowed to continue for a single day. They know that it has also been enjoined by Christ and his apostles; that without it all things are empty, with it all are fulfilled. (33)

In 388-90 Augustine and Alypius returned to Thagaste via Carthage as servants of God, that is, good Christian laymen living in the house of a pious churchman. Semi-monastic, they resembled the families of ascetics in Rome and Africa described above by Augustine. In their striving for perfection in community they were the predecessors of the monks. Augustine and Alypius moved into Augustine's family home in Thagaste, starting a small community of *servi dei* there including Adeodatus, Evodius and a few others. Augustine promptly sold most of the family property, giving the money to the poor. They spent their days praying, fasting, meditating and studying. When Augustine encouraged others to join (L 157), Severus came, but Nebridius died as he was preparing to be with them. As the little group grew in numbers, Augustine had to enlarge the house.

These servants of God appeared differently to different people. For example, Augustine describes them to Nebridius as "*deificari in otio* (leisurely worshippers)" and not just a philosophical study club as at Cassiciacum.

At Thagaste Augustine was faced with two real problems that were to affect his whole life, namely, the antagonism of the Manicheans and the Donatists, and the fear that he would be drafted for a bishopric. Thus he was careful to avoid towns in which the episcopal chair was vacant.

When Adeodatus and Nebridius died, Augustine was shaken up, determining to organize the community beyond their present leisurely contemplation. Gradually the servants of God took on a monastic hue with Augustine as superior and a semblance of order.

When Augustine went to Hippo in 391 to talk to a friend about his vocation, the people drafted him for the presbyterial office, so great was his reputation in learning and piety. Although he submitted humbly to the will of the people, Augustine always remained a monk at heart.

At Hippo with Bishop Valerius' permission, Augustine founded a monastery in the episcopal garden for his servants of God, living according to the rule established by the apostles with the main emphasis on community life, like the early Christians. This had been Augustine's ideal ever since his projected philosophical study club in Milan, which had been forestalled by the *mulierculae*. All things were to be held in common with no one having anything for himself, but only receiving what was needed from the one in charge. This had been their practice also at Thagaste.

One of the main attractions of religious communism for Augustine was the mutual support of the brethren along the hard road to chastity, for he knew his own weakness for the fairer sex. Since married priests and bishops were still common, Augustine and his friends could preserve their continence by the safeguard of the common life, with the brethren keeping an eye on each other, giving good example and encouragement.

Augustine was joined in his Hippo community by Alypius and Evodius from Thagaste, Possidius, his biographer, and others (L 158). Since Augustine always remained a professional educator, his monastery soon became a center of learning, training many of his followers to be presbyters and bishops in neighboring dioceses.

With the blessing of his bishop, Augustine preached, taught and catechized. For example, he impressed the assembled bishops at the Council of Hippo (393) with his address on Faith and the Creed. His community not only received the full support of Valerius, but also of Aurelius, archbishop of Carthage and primate of Africa. Many intelligent government officials and well-educated Romans joined, in contrast to the simple local Donatist and Catholic clerics. Already was beginning the exodus of the intelligentsia from Rome to Africa in the face of the collapsing empire. Paulinus of Nola would see in Augustine's community the kernel of a revolution in African church history as Augustine and his intellectual friends began to occupy the African sees.

Even after he was consecrated bishop in 395-96 Augustine continued to live with his community in the episcopal house, which served as a center of contemplation, catechesis, a teaching seminary and a parish hub. Always the rhetorician, Augustine had his clerical students learn secular authors, the Bible and church writers.

Augustine's community differed radically from the lay monasteries of the East. He and his servants of God by force of circumstances had become clerics, the predecessors of the later clerical orders and canons, and in a sense the whole pattern of the Western clergy, celibate, reciting office, living in rectories for mutual support. Other contemporary Western bishops had fostered clerical communism, for example, Eusebius of Vercelli, Martin of Tours, Ambrose of Milan, Victricius of Ruen, Paulinus of Nola, Germain of Anxerre. Augustine also founded monasteries for lay men and lay women, his sister ruling over the latter with his guidance.

Augustine never lorded his authority over his community, but rather ruled by charity, assisted by deacons in charge of the refectory, laundry, library and infirmary. He accepted all classes of applicants, rich and poor. While the rich should practice humility, the poor should not use their new status to stimulate their pride. All should keep busy with physical and intellectual work to support themselves.

Clothing, food and other necessities in Augustine's home were of modest proportions. And although his table was generally frugal, he served vegetables, meat and herbs for guests and the sick. Moreover, he always offered wine, as Possidius writes, "because he knew and taught, as the apostle says, 'Every creature of God is good and nothing is to be rejected that is received with thanksgiving. For it is sanctified by the word of God and prayer.'"[1] He also quoted Paul's advice to Timothy, namely, that a little wine is good for the stomach (1 Tim 5:23). Probably his life at Hippo did not differ greatly from that at Thagaste and Cassiciacum, except for an occasional feast for visiting prelates. Also his sister would sometimes send over goodies from her convent in thanks for the services of Augustine and his community.

---

1. *Life of Augustine* 12.

At table Augustine the teacher preferred reading and discussion to idle chatter. He had a plaque placed over the table, forbidding gossip. "Whoever loves to rip the lives of absent brethren, let him know that this table is not for him."[1] When one of his episcopal friends violated the rule, Augustine corrected him, saying that either the motto should be taken down or Augustine would leave the meal.

Augustine's companions wore a black habit with a cincture and a chasuble in bad weather. They shaved their heads and visited the public baths only to wash the sick and then in the presence of companions.

Augustine kept a strict cloister, for he knew his own weakness for the ladies and, no doubt, remembered how the girls had broken up his early plans in Milan. He did not even allow his widowed sister and his servant of God nieces to enter his house, although the canons allowed close relatives to live with clerics. Like the desert fathers, Augustine feared that if he allowed his sister and her daughters to move in, they would require female servants as well. And not only would he and his clerical companions be tempted, but also there would be a wagging of tongues. Augustine never spoke to a woman without a clerical witness present. Since the union of the sexes is a natural state, any attempt at separation must be surrounded by hedges of all sorts. Early Western councils at Rome (386), c. 9; Turin (398), c. 8; Toledo (400), c. 1; Carthage (401), c. 4, were constantly concerned with clerical continence based at least partially on Jewish and Roman sacerdotal customs.[2] Since clerical marriage was still in practice, probably many of Augustine's clerics were separated from their wives as Augustine had parted from his consort.

Since he left the care of the church and house to capable assistants, Augustine was free to devote himself more to contemplation and intellectual pursuits according to his earliest dreams in Milan.

Also following the Milan ideal, Augustine insisted on the community of goods according to the Acts of the Apostles (4:32). "Now the company of those who believed were of one heart and one soul, and no one said that anything he possessed was his own, but they had everything in common." Any violations of this spirit were handled severely in the light of Peter's judgment of Ananias and Sapphira (Acts 5:1-11). In other words, in handing over one's property, nothing should be held back — a complete commitment and perfect renunciation.

In sermons 355 and 356 Augustine explains to his people the rigors of his clerical commune according to the apostolic norms.

---

1. " *Quisquis amat dictis absentum rodere vitam, hanc mensam indignam noverit esse sibi,*" *Life of Augustine* 22.
2. See J. Mohler, *Origin and Evolution of the Priesthood* (New York: Alba House, 1970), *passim.*

The common life's exemplar is found among the first Christians. Augustine's monastery was first in the garden, then in the episcopal house. In a humble place safety is found, but in a high place, danger. Since the monastic life is in common, to hold anything as one's own is forbidden. I will not hold you long, since I am sitting, while you stand. All, or at least most of you, know that we so live in the episcopal house as far as possible imitating the saints spoken of in the Acts of the Apostles (4:32). (S 355)

Augustine goes on to give an apology of his monastic way.

I who by the grace of God am your bishop, came as a young man to this city, as many of you know. I was looking for a place to start a monastery to live with my brothers, leaving every hope of the world and cutting off my options. I certainly did not seek to be what I am. "I would rather be a door keeper in the house of my God than dwell in the tents of wickedness" (Ps 84:10). Although I cut myself off from those who love the world, I did not make myself equal to the rulers of the people. Nor did I choose a higher place in the Lord's banquet, but a lower one. And it pleased him to say, rise up higher . . .
I began to collect brothers of good intention, my equals, having nothing, as I had nothing. They imitated me. As I sold my small property and gave it to the poor, so did those who desired to be with me so that we could live in common. Together we possessed a large and productive estate, namely, God himself . . .
See how we live. It is not permitted in our society for anyone to have anything of his own. But perhaps some do have their own things, though this is not permitted. But if they have them, they act illicitly. I like my brothers and always believe well of them so I try to avoid any sort of inquisition, which would seem bad to me.

Although all the brothers knew of the agreement, some did not practice strict poverty. For example, Januarius, a presbyter, kept his property against the law of the monastery. He held back some money which he said was for his daughter who was in a convent. He actually made a will as he approached death, but Augustine would not accept his inheritance in the name of the church. Violators of poverty were sent away from the monastery, but not deprived of their clerical state, for to simulate the agreement of sanctity is worse than to abandon it.

Like all the church fathers, Augustine always quoted scriptures on behalf of his decisions and in defense of his way of life. Besides the passage from the Acts of the Apostles (4:32) about having all things in common Augustine found a favorite patristic theme in Psalm 132 (N).[1]

> Behold how good and pleasant it is when brothers dwell in unity. It is like precious oil upon the head, running down upon the beard, upon the beard of Aaron, running down the collar of his robes. It is like the dew of Hermon, which falls upon the mountains of Zion. For there the Lord has commanded blessing, life for ever more.

Augustine applies this beautiful psalm to the monks:

> These same words of the psalter, this sweet sound that honeyed melody, even begot the monasteries. By this sound were stirred up the brethren who longed to dwell together. This verse was their trumpet. It sounded through the whole earth, and they who had been divided were gathered together.

The early Christians answered the call, holding all things in common. Augustine continues:

> Since the psalm says, "Behold how good and pleasant it is when brothers dwell in unity" why then should we not call monks so? For *monos* is "one." Not one in any manner, since a man in a crowd is one, but though he can be called one along with others, he cannot be *monos,* that is, alone, as to make one man, so that they really possess what is written "One mind and one heart" (Acts 4:32), many bodies, but not many minds; many bodies, but not many hearts, they can rightly be called *monos,* that is, one alone. (5)

The ointment of the Holy Spirit descended on the beard of Aaron, on the Christian apostles. So the dew of Christ makes a monk peaceable, quiet, submissive, prayerful and not murmuring like noisy cartwheels bearing their burden of straw. True, the murmurers dwell together, but only in body. Those who really dwell together are of one mind and heart towards God (Eccl 33:5). "Because there the Lord commanded blessing. Where did he command it? Among the brethren who dwell together. There he enjoined blessing, there they who dwell with one heart bless God, for you bless not God in division of heart" (9).

---

1. See Basil, *Long Rule* 7.

Unity is the very essence of the monastery as it is in the church. Just as the early Fathers from Paul to Clement and Ignatius urged church unity, so Augustine and monastic founders before and after counseled unity among the monks. And whenever he found a brother disrupting the community, he asked him to leave. For example, Boniface accused a younger monk, Spes, of making disgusting propositions. But when Spes turned the tables, Boniface resigned from the community to avoid a greater scandal, although Augustine kept his name on the diptychs. Nevertheless a large scandal arose over this matter in Hippo.

African monasticism had its dissident elements. Some monk-like enthusiasts were the Donatist circumcellions, wandering from place to place without home or rule. They resemble the gyrovagi, the roadrunners of the East, who may have been the descendants of the earlier peripatetic prophet-apostles. Councils and Fathers cried out against the circumcellions who, in their defense of Donatus, robbed, beat and did violence under the pretext of religion. Augustine writes, "I see indeed marvelous works, the daily violences of the circumcellions (*circum cellas rusticorum ientes*), with the bishops and presbyters for their leaders, flying about in every direction, and calling their terrible clubs 'Israels' which men now living see and feel."[1] They spared no one, not even their own people, depriving them of their civil rights, robbing, injuring, torturing, throwing vinegar and lime into their eyes. They were especially vindictive toward the Donatists who converted to the Catholic Church. Petilian, one of their leaders, calumniated the monasteries, accusing Augustine as the founder of African monasticism.[2]

The Work of the Monks

About the year 400 Aurelius, archbishop of Carthage, asked Augustine to write against a growing monastic problem in Carthage and perhaps elsewhere, namely, wandering monks, who seem to have been orthodox in contrast to the anarchistic circumcellions. Rejecting the established manner of life which included working for a living, they preferred to beg, relying on the Lord according to Matthew (6:26), "Look to the birds of the air. They neither sow nor reap nor gather into barns, and yet their heavenly father feeds them." True nomads,

---

1. On Psalm 10 (11), 5. Also On Psalm 54 (55), 25; On Psalm 132 (133), 3; *Life of Augustine* 10.
2. *Against the Letters of Petilian* 3, 48.

wandering from place to place, they sold relics, begging, with long hair and disheveled appearance. Many examples of shipwrecked lives joined their ranks.

Paul, writing to the millennial Thessalonians (2 Thes 3:10), said, "If any man will not work, let him not eat." However, lazy monks took this in a spiritual sense so that they could avoid boring and tiring physical labor with impunity. But Augustine argues in his *On the Work of the Monks* (F) that Paul's own example as a hardworking tentmaker taught his followers to labor for a living.

> For you yourselves know how you ought to imitate us. We were not idle when we were with you; we did not eat anyone's bread without paying. But with toil and labor we worked night and day, that we might not burden any of you. It was not because we have not that right, but to give you in our conduct an example to imitate, for even when we were with you, we gave you this command: if anyone will not work, let him not eat. For we hear that some of you are living in idleness, mere busybodies, not doing any work. Now such persons we command and exhort in the Lord Jesus Christ to do their work in quietness and to earn their own living. Brethren, do not be weary of well-doing.

It seems that some of the Thessalonians, perhaps misinterpreting the earlier directives of Paul, were sitting around idly awaiting the imminent eschaton.

Although Paul could have lived off the gospel as the other apostles did and as the Lord permitted, he chose rather to earn his own way as a tentmaker (12-13). In this he observed the talmudic tradition in which the rabbis worked at their trade in the morning and taught in the afternoon. Jesus and his disciples may well have followed this pattern. The lazy monks, however, claim that they need leisure for prayer, psalmody, reading and preaching. But they can chant while working (17). Augustine is sympathetic with the wealthy monks who are not used to manual labor. But also those from peasant backgrounds seek to avoid work.

> In this Christian campaign for holiness, the rich are not humiliated so that the poor can be lifted up to haughtiness. It is not at all fitting that, in a mode of life where senators become laborers, workmen should become men of leisure; that peasants should be pampered in the monastery to which those who were masters of estates have abandoned all their goods. (25)

It seems that the plebians and even slaves were sometimes drawn toward the monastic life of ease, and since monkhood was an honor, for them it was a step up the social ladder. The monks, then, should not tempt God by their indolence.

If through any infirmity or occupation we are not able to work, God feeds and clothes us as he provides for the birds and the lilies which perform no labor of this sort. But, when we are able to work, we ought not to tempt our God, because it is by his gift that we are able to do what we do, and because, while we live on this earth, we live by his bounty, since he has made our existence possible. (27)

Augustine criticizes the hypocrites who go around in monks' garb, wandering through the provinces without home or stable existence. Some sell relics, real or spurious. Others enlarge their fringes or phylacteries like the Pharisees. Still others say that they are searching for their parents or relatives whom they have heard are living in distant places, begging rewards for their destitution and pretended piety. When apprehended for their evil ways, they discredit the whole family of monks.

Embarrassed by his own situation, Augustine apologizes that he is too busy to do manual labor and sometimes feels too weak physically.

So far as I am concerned, I would much prefer to do some manual labor at certain hours each day as is the custom in well-regulated monasteries and to have other hours free for reading, prayer or for the study of sacred scriptures than to endure the very confusing perplexities of the problems of others in regard to worldly concerns which must be eliminated by our judgments or curtail our action. (29)

Not only are the lazy monks tolerated, but are acclaimed as more righteous for their indolence. "So that monasteries established on wholesome principles are corrupted by a twofold evil, the lazy license of leisure and the unmerited name of holiness" (30).

Many of these monks, anti-social and lazy, also sported long flowing locks. And their Samson's manes drove some people wild. True, the Nazarites, the early Jewish predecessors of the monks, let their hair grow and, indeed, some of the Eastern Christian monks did likewise. However, the custom was repugnant to clean-shaven Romans. Paul warned, "For a man to wear his hair long is degrading" (1 Cor 11:14). But the recalcitrant monks claimed that this did not apply to them since they were not men, but eunuchs for Christ. Nevertheless, though Paul was also a eunuch for Christ, he still advocated short hair.

Augustine mourned that now even some of the good monks were adopting the new style. However, they should cease lest they give scandal and cause contentions (33).

Augustine and the Virgins

Another and more serious problem in monasticism was the increasing attacks on virginity. For example, Jovinian, an ex-monk, preaching against the monastic way in the latter part of the fourth century, persuaded many monks and nuns to abandon their calling.

Jovinian claimed that those who advocated virginity were not saying anything different from the Manicheans who condemned marriage. There is no doubt that there were parallels between heterodox dualism, disdaining the flesh and marriage, and orthodox asceticism. In general, however, the orthodox looked upon human passions not as evil, but rather good, though weakened and prone to sin.

Since Jovinian felt that his accusations could only be answered by a condemnation of marriage, Augustine wrote first his treatise *On the Good of Marriage* (401) and then his work *On Holy Virginity* (401). Because Jovinian had attacked Mary's virginity, claiming that she lost it in the birth of Christ, Augustine started out in her defense, teaching that Mary was a vowed virgin who remained so throughout life. Moreover, she is the virgin mother of the church, which is Christ's body. Furthermore, the virginal church is spiritually the mother of Christ in his members through baptism. Likewise the consecrated virgin of the church has a spiritual motherhood in union with Christ by bringing souls to eternal life in charity.

In the second part of his defense of virginity Augustine urges the Christian virgins to follow the Lamb wherever he goes (Rv 12:2-4).

> Press on, then, saints of God, youths and maidens, men and women, celibates and virgins, press on unflaggingly toward the goal. Praise the Lord more sweetly, to whom your thoughts are more fully devoted! Hope in him more eagerly, whom you serve more eagerly. Love him more ardently whom you please more carefully, with loins girt, and lamps lit, await the Lord, when he returns from the wedding. (27) (F)

Follow the virginal Lamb away from the deceits of the world to far-reaching and difficult pastures.

However, Augustine warns, "Many things in him are proposed to all for imitation, but virginity of the flesh is not proposed for all for there is nothing they can do to become virgins whom it has befallen not to be virgins" (28). Although the multitude of the faithful will not be able to follow, they will rejoice with the virgins in following the Lamb, not avoiding a forbidden marriage, but rising above a lawful one. Yet the virgin must imitate the humble Christ, avoiding all tendencies to pride (31).

Augustine chastises the false virgins who really want to marry but do not out of fear of scandal or notoriety (34). Others dress in a worldly and immodest manner with unusual headdresses and fancy hairdos showing through thin veils and are proud of their calling.

Christ is the model of virginal integrity and humility. It was not iniquity but charity that made him humble. A virgin should always live in humble fear lest she fall from her vocation. "Is it to be thought that God permits that many men and women who will fall away be included in the ranks of your profession for anything else than that by their fall your fear may be increased and by it pride may be crushed?" (40).

This brings up the important relationship of virginity and widowhood to marriage. Which is better? What about the virgin who leaves her special calling in order to marry? Is she not choosing an inferior way? Some even accused her of adultery. Augustine responds in his letter to Juliana.[1]

The marriages of such persons are not in themselves deserving of condemnation. What is condemned is the abandonment of purpose, the violation of the vow; not the choice of an inferior good, but the fall from a higher good. Finally, such persons are condemned, not for having contracted marriage, but for having broken their first troth of continence. (9)

However, he would not accuse them of adultery.

It is impossible for me to admit that women who marry after abandoning a more perfect state do not contract a valid marriage, but commit adultery. I do not hesitate to say plainly that the abandonment and the violation of a holier chastity pledged to the Lord is worse than adultery. If we must believe that it is an offense against Christ for one of his members to be unfaithful to her husband, how much more grievous is the offense when faith is not kept with him in the observance of that chastity which he claims when it has been offered, but which he did not require

---

1. *On the Good of Widowhood* (414) (F). When the Roman Vestal Virgins violated their vows, they were put to death!

to be offered. The iniquity of infidelity to the vow, which was made not by force of command, but by the invitation of a counsel, is increased by the fact that there was no necessity in the first place to make the vow that has been broken. (11)[1]

Let us return to Augustine's exhortation on virginity where he continues to urge humility. "Let the first thought of the virgin of God be to be filled with humility lest she think that it comes to her from herself that she is such and not think rather that this best gift comes from above" (41). Wisdom is necessary to recognize continence as a gift of God. "Whoever remains chaste from the beginning is ruled by him, and whoever is made chaste from impurity is corrected by him, and whoever is unchaste to the very end is abandoned by him" (42). All of this he accomplishes by a mysterious judgment to increase fear on our part and diminish our pride.

Like the Roman Vestals, the Christian virgins were honored in the liturgy and outside as well. However, the virgin must humbly acknowledge God's gift and not exalt herself over others. Moreover, this is to be real humility, for mock meekness is worse than presumptuous pride. Although virginity should be considered as a higher calling than marriage, "nevertheless, let not this or that obedient and God-fearing virgin presume to set herself above this or that obedient and God-fearing wife. For otherwise she will not be humble, and God resists the proud" (44). The virgin should be the chaste symbol of the pure church united to her divine Spouse. Let the virgins follow the Lamb in purity, truthfulness and humility (49), for he will exalt those who follow him humbly (52).

There had been many letters and treatises on virginity by John Chrysostom, Ambrose, Jerome and others. But Augustine's tract seems so balanced, especially when seen alongside his work *On the Good of Marriage*. Not a virgin himself, Augustine was perhaps better able to evaluate virginity objectively as a gift humbly received and not a Pelagian victory of the will over the sex appetites.

There were many convents of virgins in North Africa in Augustine's day. Since Roman women, in general, were not allowed in the professions, the convents were logical gathering places for old maids, widows and virgins. Some young nuns were freed slave girls, while others were daughters of the rich. Many of these religious houses were family monasteries, headed by a widow with some of her daughters

---

1. Augustine's dim view of those who choose to leave the state of ecclesiastical virginity should be seen in the light of the severe punishments given to the Roman Vestal Virgins who reneged on their vocation.

and other female relatives and friends making up the community. Marcella's and Paula's foundations in Rome come to mind.

Augustine's Rule

Augustine's own widowed sister headed a convent in Hippo, another example of the brother and sister combinations which sparkle throughout the history of monasticism. When his sister retired as superioress, the new abbess encountered some opposition, evidently after ruling for some time. In 423 Augustine wrote a letter to the community (L 211) urging them not to remove their leader who had been in the convent so long, who had trained many of them and loved them like a mother. Was their new spiritual director at fault? If so, he probably was a member of Augustine's own community.

The first part of the letter (1-4) is an *objurgatio* or reproof of the erring sisters. Since the earliest manuscripts follow this with "explicit," *Augustine's Rule* (5-16) which follows may have been a later addition to the letter. But it very likely was the rule obeyed by his community and, mutatis mutandis, also by his sister's convent. It is more a mode of conduct than an organized rule.

Above all, Augustine pleads for unity, having all things in common, with the superior distributing food and clothing according to need (Acts 4:32, 35). The rich nuns should turn in their possessions to the common stock. Poorer members should not be puffed up, while the more wealthy ones should not look down on their less privileged sisters.

Prayer is essential to the religious life and it should be celebrated at the proper time in the oratory, meditating on the verses of scriptures. Fasting and abstinence are encouraged with due regard for health. Reading should be had at table so that soul and body can be nourished together.

However, due care should be had for those who are used to delicate fare and a more luxurious way of life, so they should be allowed modifications in food, dress, bedding, etc. Moreover, the hardy peasants should not be jealous of the weaker rich girls. This double standard may have led to the contentions mentioned above.

The clothing of the sisters should be modest with a net covering their hair. When they go out, they are to be accompanied by a companion. "If your eyes glance at anyone, let them rest upon no one, for you are not forbidden to look at men when you go out, but to desire them or to wish to be desired by them is wrong." The unchaste eye is the messenger of the unchaste heart. Although she may escape the notice of men, the Observer from above sees all. The nun with a wandering glance should be corrected in a sisterly manner.

Clothing should be especially cared for by those in charge. Religious should not be concerned about wearing some one else's dress from the common stock. However, if a sister insists on wearing the same garments she had before, at least they should be kept in the common room when not in use. The common good must always precede that of the individual so that any gifts from relatives or friends must be turned in for the use of all.

Clothes should be regularly washed, but not abstemiously so. Baths may be taken once a month, and for the sick more often. They should go to the public baths with companions according to the choice of the superior. And those put in charge of the storeroom, wardrobe and library should serve conscientiously without complaint.

Quarrels should be avoided wherever possible and when they do pop up should be quickly reconciled. For the sister who never asks pardon has no place in the monastery. Mutual love should be the norm, but without any carnal overtones.

The superior should be obeyed like a mother and should not fail to correct when needed. In matters outside of her jurisdiction she should consult with the chaplain. "Let her esteem herself happy, not in having power to rule, but in having charity to serve. Let her be set over you in honor before men; before God let her be beneath your feet." She should reprimand the loud, while encouraging the feeble-minded and weak — above all be patient, seeking rather to be loved than to be feared. The sisters, on their part, should be obedient and considerate, realizing that the position of superior has a higher risk.

> May the Lord grant you to observe these relations with love, as souls whose affections are set on spiritual beauty, whose good conduct is fragrant with the good order of Christ, not as a bondswoman under the law, but as a free woman established under grace.

These rules should be read aloud to all once a week in order to keep them fresh in mind.

Several rules today carry the name of Augustine. Besides the *Regula Puellarum* (RP) of L 211, there is the *Regula Virorum* (RV), probably the original rule of Augustine's monastery in Hippo, the *Regula Consensoria* (C) from the sixth to the eighth century in Spain and the *Disciplina Monasterii* (DM) written by Augustine for the monks at Thagaste. *Augustine's Rule* (RV) is cited by Caesarius of Arles (sixth century), Benedict, Isadore of Seville, Benedict of Aniane and others. Moreover, it was used by European canons from the eleventh century.

Approved by the Fourth Lateran Council (1198-1216), it was adopted by Dominic Guzman and also by the thirteenth century Augustinians. No less than 150 religious groups follow Augustine's rule today. And each renewal of religious life through the centuries is often accompanied by a rebirth of the Augustinian spirit.

In conclusion, we have seen that Augustine, like the philosophers of old, was inclined to a common life of leisure, contemplating the truth. He had planned it at Milan and come close to it at Cassiciacum. After his conversion he became sold on monasticism, inspired by the *Life of Antony* and the monks of Milan and Rome. He and his fellow servants of God led a semi-monastic regimen in his family home at Thagaste. When he was elected presbyter and bishop of Hippo, he continued his monastic way, turning the bishop's house into a clerical-seminary-monastery. Augustine did much to defend and correct African monasticism, the results of which can still be seen in the customs of Western clergy and religious.

In the following chapter we will see the problem of divine grace and human free will, and its relationship to the monastic tradition and how Augustine debated the matter with Pelagius, John Cassian and others.

VII.

THE GRACE OF GOD IS ALWAYS GOOD

(On Grace and Free Will, 1)

Augustine and Pelagius

Another problem that arose from the monk-like servants of God, stimulating Augustine's problem-centered theology, was the teachings of Pelagius. Probably from Britain or Ireland, this peripatetic servant of God made his mark in Rome, Carthage and Jerusalem. His principle of self-discipline was the cornerstone of ascetical practice going back to the *apeitheia* (apathy) of the Stoics, Origen and Evagrius. In this struggle for perfection Pelagianism, asceticism and monasticism had something in common.

The history of asceticism seems to balance between the radicals and the orthodox. For example, the Encratists, Montanists, Euchites, Donatists, Pelagians, all seeking perfection were highly critical of the mores of the contemporary church. Like many of these, Pelagius exaggerated innate human goodness and capabilities for perfection. Monasticism, of course, had similar origins and ambitions, but was kept within bounds by men like Antony, Athanasius, Pachomius, Basil, Jerome, Augustine, John Cassian, Benedict and others.

Pelagius came to Rome from Britain a little before Augustine arrived there. He was highly virtuous, ascetic, well-educated, an excellent writer and esteemed by many. Some such as Paulinus of Nola, Sulpicius Severus and Juliana thought he was a saint. And later when Augustine and Jerome were criticizing him, eighteen Italian bishops rose to his defense.

In the new ascetical movement of the times prominent and sometimes wealthy men and women put their palaces at the disposal of great ascetics such as Jerome, Augustine and Pelagius. The latter joined his rich friends in studying Paul, writing letters to encourage their asceticism. There is evidence that there was a certain rivalry for the direction of the rich widows.

Pelagius' rigorous tenet was: if perfection is possible, it is obligatory.

With no doubts about human capabilities, he felt that by the use of our free will and a certain Stoic asceticism we might reach a state where we would be beyond sinning. Since human nature is a gift of God and basically good, we are free to choose between good and evil and so ultimately achieve salvation. Pelagius is basically anti-Manichean. This is why he admires Augustine's anti-Manichean work *On Free Choice,* which he quotes in his *On Nature* which is an argument against the toleration of sin as human weakness.

Fleeing the sack of Alaric (410), Pelagius embarked to Africa for a brief stay, then on to the Holy Land, while his disciple Coelestius remained behind to stir up Africa, challenging the heredity of Adam's sin and the necessity of infant baptism. His teachings were condemned by the bishops at Carthage in 411.

As we have seen, the barbarian invasions had an effect on Roman life of the period, urging flights to Africa and Palestine, and prompting a lively interest in religious life as an alternative in the chancy times of the barbarian onslaughts.

Pelagius had many followers who read and circulated his letters and works, forming Pelagian study clubs in many places throughout the empire. With Christianity mediocre and invasions imminent, the ground was well prepared for Pelagius' seeds. As Brown comments.

> While some might be driven into retirement by such catastrophes, the Pelagians seemed determined to turn outwards, to reform the whole Christian church. This is the remarkable feature of their movement. The narrow stream of perfectionism that had driven the noble followers of Jerome to Bethlehem and had led Paulinus to Nola and Augustine from Milan to a life of poverty in Africa, is suddenly turned outwards in the Pelagian writings to embrace the whole Christian church.[1]

In his ceaseless striving for perfection Pelagius wanted all Christians to be monks.[2] And in this he resembled the Euchites and later some Renaissance reformers.

Augustine saw in Pelagius' zeal for a perfect church a similarity to Donatism which claimed to be the true, pure and uncorrupted Christianity. Brown remarks, "The victory of Augustine over Pelagius was also a victory for the average good Catholic layman of the later empire over an austere, reforming ideal."[3] Augustine preferred his ordinary believing Roman Christian who sometimes had intercourse

---

1. *Augustine of Hippo* (Berkeley: UCP, 1967), 347.
2. *To Demetrias* 10.
3. *Augustine of Hippo* 348.

with his wife just for the pleasure of it and who was given to anger and quibbling with his neighbors over property rights, to Pelagius' ascetic without faith.[1]

Pelagius' disciples such as Juliana, Melania the Younger and Pinian had broken with Roman society by sheer will power. They felt that the evils of the Roman world lay not within human nature, which was good, but in the external society in need of reform. Job was the hero of the Pelagians, asserting his rugged individuality against evil contemporary society. Pelagius tried to persuade his rich Roman friends to abandon their wealth, giving all to the poor. But when Melania and Pinian fled to Africa, Aurelius, Augustine and Alypius persuaded them to endow monasteries rather than give all to the destitute.

Whereas Pelagius had placed all his emphasis on human responsibility for sin, Augustine was more realistic, reflecting his own experience, in stressing innate human weakness. Answering Pelagius' *On Nature,* Augustine wrote his *On Nature and Grace* (415), asserting that our nature, due to the fall of Adam, is weak and sinful and so in need of grace to reconcile us to God and lead us to righteousness. Moreover, this grace is not given because of any human right, but purely out of God's graciousness. Pelagius, on the other hand, thought that it was possible to live without sin, since human nature had not been weakened by sin. However, Augustine accused him of replacing grace by nature. Human nature, wrote Augustine, is weakened by sin and so is slanted toward sin without the help of divine grace. Furthermore, by minimizing the necessity of grace and the church, Pelagius had lessened the distinction between a good Christian and a good pagan.

It was the adverse influence of Pelagius that prompted Augustine to write to the widow Juliana of the influential family of Anicius Probus.[2] When her father-in-law Probus died, her mother-in-law Proba had consecrated her widowhood to God, founding a community of widows and virgins in Rome. She was known to both Augustine and Jerome and along with Proba defended the cause of John Chrysostom.

When Alaric invaded Rome (410), Proba, Juliana and Juliana's daughter Demetrias fled to Carthage where they were promptly imprisoned by Count Heraclian, who forced them to pay a huge tax. Juliana entered her mother's community, and when Demetrias also joined at the urging of Augustine (L 188), the Roman world was amazed. At the request of Juliana, Pelagius wrote to Demetrias to encourage her in her vocation. Angry that Pelagius was invading his field of spiritual guidance of rich widows, Jerome implied that Pelagius

---

1. *Against Two Letters of the Pelagians* 3, 14 (420).
2. *On the Excellence of Widowhood* (314).

was only after their money (L 133). The Code of Theodosius would take a dim view of clergy who milked rich widows.

Augustine, writing *On the Excellence of Widowhood,* warns Juliana about Pelagius, without mentioning him by name. However, she never lost her admiration for her mentor. She replies:

> Your priesthood knows that I and my little household are far removed from persons of that kind. All our family follow the Catholic faith so closely that we have never fallen into any heresy, nor even lapsed into any sect which seems to have even small errors, much less those which are outside the pale.[1]

Besides the advice on virginity and widowhood mentioned above, Augustine cautioned the little community that their decision to give themselves to Christ was not self-made due to their own strength of character, as Pelagius had suggested, but rather a divine calling to a more blessed life, urging them to lead others by their good example and to read thoroughly his own work *On Holy Virginity.*

Although Pelagianism seemed to have been laid to rest by Augustine and Jerome, Councils at Carthage (416) and Melvis (418), and popes Innocent I and Zozimus, we find the Anti-Pelagian writings of Augustine causing consternation in the monasteries a decade or so later. As we have seen, Pelagianism had much in common with monasticism, especially the Origenist-Evagrian line in which the monk hopes to attain perfection by virtue of his austerities and spiritual exercises much as an athlete trains himself for the games. Many monasteries around the Mediterranean such as Hadrumetum in Africa, Marseilles and Lerins in Gaul reflected these Eastern trends. Moreover, many of them, in monastic tradition, were either ignorant of or opposed to the episcopal decisions and writings.

For example, two monks from Hadrumetum, Florus and Felix, on a visit to Uzala came upon a copy of Augustine's Anti-Pelagian letter to Sixtus (L 194) (418), stressing the necessity of divine grace, human weakness and predestination. Since bishop Evodius of Uzala had been a disciple of Augustine, he undoubtedly had many of his mentor's works in his library. Making a copy of the letter, the two monks brought it back to Hadrumetum, where the community was horrified by Augustine's views on predestination, which, they felt, destroyed free will.

Abbot Valentinus of Hadrumetum promptly wrote to Evodius and also to a presbyter Januarius, seeking advice in the matter. Evodius replied affirming free will, but maintaining that it had been weakened

---

1. Quoted in Augustine's L 188 (418).

by original sin. We can freely chose God, but only when we are aided by his grace. Also Evodius recommended intellectual humility in these puzzling conundrums.

Some of the monks of Hadrumetum went right to Augustine for advice. In reply he wrote letters 214 and 215 and also his work *On Grace and Free Choice,* showing that God's grace is perfectly compatible with free will. For God works in our heart to incline our will whichever way he wishes.

> The grace of God is always good and by it it comes to pass that a man is of good will, though he was before of an evil one. By it also it comes to pass that the very good will which has now begun to be, is enlarged, and made so great that it is able to fulfill the divine commandments which it shall wish, when it shall once firmly and perfectly wish. (31)

However, one of the monks retorted that if God controls our will, there is no guilt on our part if we sin. Rather than correcting a sinner, we should pray that he receives the right grace from God. Augustine responded with his *On Rebuke and Grace* (427). Since God's will is inscrutable, we cannot fathom his gifts. Because we do not know who is predestined and who is not, we should rebuke all who sin lest they perish and drag others down with them.

But, as Brown comments, Augustine never intended his predestination to lead to quietism.

> A monk might waste his leisure worrying about his ultimate identity. To Augustine, such anxiety was misplaced. A doctrine of predestination divorced from action, was inconceivable to him. He had never written to deny freedom, merely to make it more effective in the harsh environment of a fallen world.[1]

Augustine and John Cassian

When a copy of Augustine's work *On Rebuke and Grace,* written originally for the monks of Hadrumetum, arrived in Gaul, it was spurned as an innovation by the Massilians, especially those from Lerins and S. Victor. These monks were not Pelagians or even Semi-Pelagians, for they rejected Pelagius as much as they did

---

1. *Augustine of Hippo* 403-404.

Augustine. More correctly they have been called Anti-Augustinians, opposing his novel teaching of predestination as against Christian tradition and undermining all human efforts toward salvation. They looked upon predestination as a case of overkill. However, they also admitted that all are somehow involved in Adam's sin and so cannot save themselves. Moreover, they accepted divine foreknowledge, but asserted that God's grace is given according to human merits and not independent of them.

Prosper of Aquitaine, a learned lay Christian of Southern Gaul, along with Hilary of Poitiers, took an active part in the controversy, writing to Augustine (LL 225, 226) that the Massilians objected to his treatise *On Rebuke and Grace* and his earlier books *Against Julianus*. The Massilian position was based on a long monastic and ascetical tradition, probably Egyptian and Evagrian in origin. Both Hilary and Prosper asked Augustine to answer the Massilians, who though fundamentally good men, had been misinformed.

One of the leaders of the Massilians was John Cassian, who probably wrote his Conference 13 in reply to Augustine's *On Rebuke and Grace*. Cassian along with his friend Germain had toured the Egyptian desert, interviewing many of the Fathers and bringing the best of Coptic spirituality back to Gaul. In his earlier writings Cassian followed the Eastern monastic line in which human effort prepared the way for God. However, we should always realize our essential dependence on God (Institutes 5, 21; 6, 18; 8, 12). "When we say that human efforts cannot of themselves secure it (perfection) without the aid of God, we thus insist that God's mercy and grace are bestowed only upon those who labor and exert themselves, and are granted (to use the apostle's expressions) to them that 'will' and 'run' (Institutes 12, 14). Ask and you shall receive, seek and you shall find, knock and it shall be opened to you (Mt 7:7)."

Although his Institutes placed more emphasis on our struggle for perfection, Cassian's Conferences balanced God and man. For example, in Conference 3, 11 Germain asks Paphnutius how we can do anything at all worthy of praise since God begins and ends all our salutary acts.

But how about the middle, asks Paphnutius. Although God gives us the opportunities for good acts, it is up to us to make good use of them.

But it is well for us to be sure that although we practice every virtue with unceasing efforts, yet with all our exertions and zeal we can never arrive at perfection. Nor is mere human diligence and toil of itself sufficient to deserve to reach the splendid reward of bliss, unless we have secured it by means of the cooperation of the Lord, and his directing our heart to what is right . . . None of the righteous are sufficient of themselves to acquire righteousness, unless every moment when they stumble and fall the divine mercy supports them with his hands, that they may not utterly collapse and perish, when they have been cast down through the weakness of free will. (Conference 3, 11)

We have no wish to do away with man's free will by what we have said, but only to establish the fact that the assistance and grace of God are necessary to it every day and hour. (Conference 3, 22)

In Conference 13 Cassian quotes Chaeremon on the necessity of God's grace for the monk.

Who, I ask, could, however fervent he might be in spirit, relying on his own strength with no praise from men, endure the squalor of the desert, and I will not say the daily lack, but the daily supply of dry bread? Who without the Lord's consolation could put up with the continual thirst for water, or deprive his human eyes of that sweet and delicious morning sleep and regularly compress his whole time of rest and repose into the limits of four hours? Who would be sufficient without God's grace to give continued attendance to reading and constant earnestness in work, receiving no advantage of present gain? (Conference 13, 6)

But sometimes Cassian taught that we are capable of the first turning toward God. "And when he sees in us some beginnings of good will, he at once enlightens it and strengthens it on toward salvation, increasing that which he himself planted or which he sees have risen from our own efforts" (Conference 13, 8). Although free will and grace appear as contraries, they really agree. For though our will may be weakened by sin, it is far from dead (Conference 13, 12). Like many of the Gaulic monks, Cassian stresses God's universal salvific will against Augustine's predestination. While it is true that some souls are lost, this is against God's wishes (Conference 13, 7).

Augustine responded to the Massilians with a treatise now divided into two books: *Predestination of the Saints* and *The Gift of Perseverance* (428-429). As Augustine finished this writing, his own eschaton approached along with that of Africa before the Vandal invasions. Although his doctrine on predestination had, indeed, shaken up the monks, to his dying day Augustine looked upon it as a message of confidence and assurance that God alone is man's salvation.

Soon after Augustine's death (430), the Massilians continued their attack with *Objections of the Gaulic Liars,* to which Prosper promptly responded (431). Prosper and Hilary even went to Rome to enlist the aid of Pope Celestine in their struggle against the Massilians. So Celestine wrote a letter to the Gaulic bishops, defending Prosper and Augustine and warning against novelties. Finally Prosper answered Cassian's Conference 13 with his *On Grace and Free Will, Against the Contributor.*

In general, however, the Anti-Augustinian school of Marseilles continued through the fifth century with Vincent of Lerins, Faustus of Riez and Gennadius. The matter was not settled until the second Council of Orange (529) under the leadership of Caesarius of Arles, strongly reasserting prevenient grace.

The resistance of the Gaulic monks to Augustine was based largely on the fear that predestination weakened the whole ascetical scheme. Why become an athlete in the games of salvation when the victory is predetermined and when our nature is so corrupt that we are in a hopeless struggle?

John Cassian died in 433, three years after Augustine. But his Institutes and Conferences continued to influence southern Gaul and were required reading for future generations of monks and religious.

John Cassian is the first Western doctor of the science of the spiritual life including mental prayer, but he also gave an impetus to the liturgy and the office. His was a moderate spirituality, better adapted to the Western temperament. Owen Chadwick remarks.

> Cassian bequeathed to Latin Christianity the idea that the spiritual life is a science in which prayer reigns; that it is possible to analyze temptation and the nature of sin; that methods of prayer and mortification are neither haphazard nor individual, but ordered according to established experience. All the guides to spirituality in which Western Europe later abounded are his direct descendants.[1]

Augustine, too, was a great Western monastic founder, as we have seen. If he objected to any type of asceticism, it was the Origenist-Evagrian-Pelagian type which seemed to put the burden on human effort toward salvation, at least in the beginning of one's spiritual life in order to achieve a certain Stoic *apeitheia*. Augustine rightly challenged: how does this differ from pagan austerity? Perhaps as some ascetics overplayed the human side, Augustine in his Anti-Pelagian

---

1. John Cassian, *A Study of Primitive Monasticism* (Cambridge University Press, 1950), 186.

works may have overstressed the part of God in salvation. Some feel that John Cassian's Conference 13 strikes a balance.

We have seen Augustine's views on marriage and religious life. In the following chapter we will study his attitude toward women who play such important roles in each of these vocations.

VIII.

THE WIFE OF ONE HUSBAND

(Confessions 9, 9)

Christian and Roman Women

Perhaps we should see a bit of background before discussing Augustine's feminology because he is a product of the Roman and Christian patriarchal system, though he worked hard to overcome the prevalent vice of male chauvinism.

McKenzie notes that the New Testament teaches principles opposing the social and legal depression of women in the East and the excessive emancipation of Roman women.[1]

Jesus led the way to the liberation of women. He had many women friends whom he taught and healed. In no place in Jesus' teaching is there any hint of misogyny or lack of respect for the female gender. Women assisted Jesus' apostolate and were always there when he needed them beginning with Mary, Elizabeth, Anna, Mary Magdalene, Mary and Martha, etc.

Jesus teaches monogamy and the indissolubility of marriage, both defending women against exploitation, sexual harassment and the double standard of polygamy and divorce (Mt 5:27-33; 22:30).

Women prophesied in the early church (1 Cor 11; 1 Cor 14:34-6; AA 18, 24-8; AA 21, 8-9), Paul is ambivalent about the prophetesses (1 Cor 11:4; 1 Cor 14:34-36; 1 Tim 2:11). In the Jewish tradition the synagogue was a male bastion. However, we can be sure that any prohibitions of women speaking out in church implies that just the opposite was happening.

Paul bases the subjection of women to men on the Adam and Eve story so popular in the millennial times of the new Adam. Though the woman's obedience to her husband is due to her garden sin, it was not that way in the beginning, nor will it be this way in the kingdom of the new Adam (1 Cor 11:11-12; Gal 3:28).

---

1. McKenzie, *Dictionary of the Bible* (Milwaukee: Bruce, 1963), 937.

Paul compares the Christian wife to the church, whose spouse is Christ. Yet the husband is the head of his wife as Christ is the head of his church (Col 3:18). And as Christ and his bride are one body, so also husband and wife (Eph 5:38).

In his eschatological times, Paul prefers virginity to marriage (1 Cor 7:39-40). Virgins were also honored in Roman and Jewish society, that is, the Vestals and the Therapeuts. Furthermore, Paul blesses the man of one wife and the woman of one husband in the Roman tradition.[1]

Early Christian writers have more praise for widows, virgins, martyrs and prophetesses, perhaps because of the *tutela mulierum* (guardianship of women) according to which the bishop would have the guardianship of the virgins and widows in the church, whereas married women would be under the guardianship of their husbands. Yet many of the Fathers laud the good Christian wife, e.g. Clement of Alexandria, Tertullian and John Chrysostom.

As the church settles down, the apostles and prophets disappear in favor of a more structured ministry. Laporte comments:

The "servant of God" replaced the prophet and the eunuch for the kingdom, and the "widow of the church" and the "holy virgin" inherited some portion of the gift of the prophetic life. Later monasticism would develop as a prophetic movement.[2]

Although originally the Christian virgins lived at home, by the fourth century convents of virgins were common. Often this was a family home, headed by a widow and including her daughters and some of their friends, devoted to the service of the church and to prayer. The millennial times of the disintegration of the Roman empire encouraged the growth of monasticism.

Deaconesses also flourished in the East, dedicated to social work among the women of the church. Probably they were an inheritance from the synagogal structure like the presbyters and deacons.

Like the Jews, Roman society was patriarchal, with the woman under the *manus* of her father or husband or under the *tutela* of an assigned guardian. Women were banned from public office.

Berger remarks:

As long as the guardianship (*tutela*) over women was in force, women were not able to conclude legal transactions or manage

---

1. See J. Mohler, *Origin and Evolution of the Priesthood* (New York: Alba House, 1969), 25.
2. *The Role of Women in Early Christianity* (New York: Mellen, 1982), 57.

their affairs without the consent of their guardian. Furthermore, women could not be guardians.

The guardianship was supposed to protect women because of their weakness and their ignorance of business and public life (*infirmitas sexus*). However, the Roman matron is the mistress of her household. She wears a purple stole and has a reserved seat in the theater. Moreover, she can testify in court and manage her own property.

By the end of the Republic no-fault divorce and consequent promiscuity were endemic, undermining the once strong Roman family. The emancipation of women was encouraged by powerful empresses such as Livia and Plotina. Many liberated women with little interest in child bearing spent more and more time in law, politics and men's sports. Carcopino writes, "By copying men too closely, the Roman women succeeded more rapidly in emulating man's vices than in acquiring his strength."[1]

While Augustus tried to abolish the double standard of adultery by equalizing the punishments for men and women, the people chose rather to imitate his easy divorce style.

Whereas in the good old days women were under the *manus* of their husbands, now they are equal to men or even over them. And while property was formerly held in common, now it is owned separately. Then women were proud of their progeny, but not now. Then women were faithful to their husbands, but now they are capricious. Then divorce was rare, but now it is frequent. Martial, like Jesus, saw divorce as a type of adultery and a deviation from the ideal of the man of one wife and the woman of one husband (6, 7, 5).[2]

Ambrose: "She Needs the Protection of a Man"

Ambrose, like the other Fathers, teaches Paul's interpretation of Genesis, that is, though Adam was created first, Eve sinned first. So as she is subject to Adam, and the wife is under her husband. Certainly the Roman *manus, patria potestas* and *tutela mulierum* (jurisdiction, patriarchal authority, guardianship of women) are influences in this doctrine, as well.

Ambrose notes that while man was created outside of Paradise, woman was made within the gates.[3] "This teaches us that each person acquires grace by reason of virtue" and not because of place or race.

---

1. *Daily Life in Ancient Rome* (London: Routledge, 1946), 92.
2. *Ibid.*, 100.
3. J. Mohler, *Paradise* (Satya Press, 1984), 4.

Since woman was first deceived and then deceived her husband, she should obey him (1 Pt 3:1). "She who was made for assistance needs the protection of man" (Gn 2:18) (*tutela mulierum*). "The head of the woman is man. While he believed he would have the help of his woman, he fell because of her" (1 Cor 11:3).

One should share his grace with his protégé. Thus a husband should dwell with his wife in a considerate manner, honoring her as the weaker vessel, "as coheir of the grace of life that your prayers be not hindered." Even before she was deceived, woman "shared grace with man because she was taken from a man." This is a great mystery (Eph 5:32).

Eve sinned with forethought and knowingly made her husband a participant in her own wrongdoing. Was cupidity the motive? Perhaps she did not want to be separated from her husband (6).

When God made man, he did not say, "It is good," as he did after his other creations (10). Rather it is *not good* for man to be alone (Gn 2:18). So after he created man and woman God saw that all was good (Gn 1:31). "The meaning is clear. The creation of both man and woman is considered to be good."

Woman is made out of Adam's rib, not out of earth. "God wanted human nature to be established as one," and not two disparate natures. "Let us make him a helper like himself" (Gn 2:18), a helper in generation.

Whose fault was the sin? (12). Some say Adam's. For "it was not Eve but Adam who received the command from God because the woman had not yet been created." Scripture does not inform us what Adam told Eve. However, Ambrose believes that the initial deceit and violation are due to the woman, since her sex is weak and liable to do wrong. Adam did not deceive Eve, but Eve, Adam (1 Tim 2:14).

Though Eve admits her sin of disobedience, yet she possesses the food of virtue, confesses, is pardoned and given a milder punishment, that is, to be under her husband, a stronger vessel and governed by his counsel. Likewise the church turns to Christ for guidance.

Like Paul, Ambrose raises up the Christian housewife by comparing her to holy mother church, the spouse of Christ. She gives birth to new members to be reborn in the church.[1]

Husband and wife have equal rights and duties for neither is allowed to violate the marriage vows (L 19). Moreover, they should put up with each other's faults.[2] Battling traditional insensitive Roman patriarchal power (*patria potestas*), Ambrose advises the husband to

---

1. *Abraham* 1, 7.
2. *Hexaemeron* 5, 7.

lay aside his extreme emotion, rudeness, and obstinacy, refusing to admit he is wrong, "when your gentle consort offers you her love." "You are not her master, but her husband." And "she is not your servant, but your wife." Be a guide and not a dictator, tempering your hardness of heart, severity and rudeness.

Furthermore, adultery is to be avoided as a serious offense. For it is cruel for a man to abandon the wife of his youth.[1]

Augustine, Adam and Eve

We have seen some of Augustine's writings on women, for example, his directives to virgins and religious (chapter 6), and wives and mothers (chapter 5).

God created one from the other, in drawing woman from the side of man in a sharing union.[2] Joined at the side, they walk together and children follow from their intimacy. But Augustine feels that there could have been friendly relations between Adam and Eve in Paradise without sex, one ruling while the other obeyed.

Eve was created as a helpmate to Adam especially in procreation.[3] For order and peace somebody has to be in charge. So God created man first and took woman from his side (11). Augustine feels that man is more spiritual minded.

Paul said that woman is the glory of man (1 Cor 11:7), "not in the sense that the woman's mind cannot receive the same image . . . because in the stage of grace there is neither male nor female" (Gal 3:28). Since the woman was first led astray, she must have less knowledge. But she would have acquired it gradually under the tutelage of her husband.

Why did Adam believe the serpent that they would become like gods when he was supposed to be so spiritual and intelligent? (Gn 3:5). And the woman was assumed to have an inferior intellect. Yet she can receive the same image of God that her husband was given (Gal 3:28). Was she to have accepted this under the guidance of Adam? Paul calls Adam a transgressor as well (Rom 5:14). Moreover, Adam does not admit that Eve led him astray, but rather says that she gave him to eat.

Augustine, like Ambrose, says that woman's submission to man and also lust and death are due to original sin.[4] In the garden there was no

---

1. *On Luke* 1, 43.
2. *The Good of Marriage* 1. Unless otherwise noted, the next few quotes are from here.
3. *Literal Interpretation of Genesis* 9.
4. *City of God* 14, 23.

lust, for the passions were under the control of the will with mutual trust and chaste love. So the husband with his energies restrained and a quiet mind embraces his lovely wife. And when the child comes there is no painful birth.

Monica

The woman who had the most influence on Augustine and her whole family was his mother Monica, a leading Roman matron in Thagaste. Perhaps we can see better the place of women in fourth century Roman society by reading the life of Monica rather than speculating on paradise, the Adam and Eve tale and Paul's interpretation. As we have seen, by the fourth century many restrictions on women had been lifted, though remnants of the old patriarchal system were still in evidence.

Monica and her husband Patricius were a mixed marriage. But as Paul says, the Christian wife consecrates her pagan spouse. Although Augustine was not baptized as a child, he was a catechumen. And though he wished to marry young like his buddies, his mother wanted him to study for a profession in Carthage. While there he fell in with the Manicheans and began living with a consort. So his mother disowned him, yet when her husband died, Monica went to live with her son and his small family.

Augustine writes of Monica with tender love in his *Confessions*. "Who brought me to birth, both in her flesh, so that I was born into this temporal light, and in her heart that I might be born into eternal life." Though well trained by her nanny, Monica began to sneak wine until corrected by a maidservant (9, 9).

Married at an early age to Patricius, Monica served him as a lord (Eph 5:21), while trying to convert him by her pious example (1 Pt 3:1). Despite his many offenses against her marriage bed, "she looked forward to seeing your mercy upon him, so that he would believe in you and be made chaste."

When her women friends complained about wife abuse, Monica would blame it on their sharp tongues. After all, the marriage contract is a form of slavery. So they should not go around putting on airs. Monica never grumbled that her husband beat her or argued against her. Rather she waited for him to calm down before trying to reason with him.

Moreover, by her patience and kindness she won over her mother-in-law and quieted the malicious gossip of the maidservants. Monica was a peacemaker and a reconciler, always speaking well of others. "She had you as her inward teacher in the school of her heart."

Finally, due to Monica's prayers and example, Patricius was converted to Christianity. Yet she never complained about what she endured while he was an unbeliever.

She was always a servant of God's servants. And whoever knew her, "greatly praised you, and honored you and loved you in her, because they recognized your presence in her heart." Monica is the ideal Christian matron, the wife of one husband, dutiful to her parents, governing her house well, full of good works, raising her children properly, while worrying over them, "being as often in labor in birth of them as she saw them straying from you." In her last days she took care of Augustine and his friends like a mother, while serving them like a daughter.

Monica mourned over her son's Manicheanism. While Augustine wallowed in the mire, this chaste, devout and sober widow wept and prayed for him. When she asked a bishop to talk with her son, he told her that Augustine was too proud to listen. However, in the end her prayers would win him over. She accompanied him to Rome, Milan and Cassiciacum where she participated in the lively philosophical discussions.

As a *mater familias* (matriarch) Monica took part in the arranging of Augustine's marriage. For she wanted him out of his *matrimonium injustum* (unequal marriage) and into a *matrimonium justum* (equal marriage) with a higher class girl in order to move up in society (6, 13). Also she hoped that once out of his concubinous union, he would be baptized.

Augustine had been faithful to his companion of thirteen years, the mother of his son Adeodatus. He wept when he put her on the boat back to Africa.

After the conversion of Augustine and his son, Monica was happy to pass to her heavenly reward. Augustine and his brother Navigius witnessed her happy death (9, 12). "In that last illness she mingled her endearments with my dutiful deeds, calling me a good son." Indeed, Augustine had always been respectful to his dear mother. Yet there was no comparison between his honor to Monica and her devotion to him.

Augustine calls his mother "The Lord's handmaid." "The devout life she led in you and her sweet and holy care for us."

She had been made to live in Christ even while not yet released from the flesh, and she had so lived as to give praise to your name by her faith and conduct.

From her baptism "no word had issued from her mouth contrary to your commandment." Yet Monica was not sinless. Still she was merciful to the faults of others. "Do you also forgive her debts, if she contracted any."

When death came, Monica desired no fancy grave or stone. "Her only wish was that she be remembered at your altar, which she had served without the loss of a single day," for from it is dispensed that Holy Victim, who blots out all sin.

"By the bond of faith your handmaid bound her soul to this sacrament of our redemption." "May she rest in peace with that husband, before whom and after whom she had no other, whom she obeyed with patience, bringing forth fruit to you so that she might win him to you."

In Monica we see the ideal Christian Roman matron, the wife of one husband, competent manager of her household, kind, virtuous, hospitable, forgiving, daily communicant, patient with her husband, praying for her wayward son.

Augustine's Letters to Women

Like many of the other Church Fathers, Augustine was a spiritual father to men and women either by spoken word or by letter. Many of his women correspondents were either widows or servants of God who had begun convents of virgins in their homes.

We have seen some of Augustine's letters to women already, that is, his letter to his sister's convent, outlining a rule for the religious life (L 211), and his message to Felicia (L 208).

Augustine wrote to the widow Proba, exiled to Africa with her family, answering some of her questions about prayer (L 130). To help her out of her depression, Augustine suggests she meditate on the persistent widow of the gospels, who did not give up (Mt 6:7-8).

Though God knows our problems, nevertheless, it helps us to voice them anyway. Augustine prefers short prayers like those of the Coptic monks. For too long prayers are boring and so leave us open to distractions. The Our Father is the ideal prayer, since it covers all our needs.

We should not rejoice when our prayers are heard or be depressed when they go unanswered. Rather we should pray for God's will. What if we do not know what to pray for? Let the Holy Spirit take over for us (Rom 8:25, 27). Finally, pray continually like the widow in the Lord's parable.

In 413 Augustine wrote to the aristocratic nun Paulina to respond to her question whether God can be seen in a visible form (L 147). When Christ dwells in us in faith, we are no longer Jew or Greek, slave or free, male or female (Gal 3:28). Do we see him inwardly or outwardly? Neither! We should just rest in scripture, where the clean of heart will see God (Mt 5:8).

On the other hand, no man has seen God (Jn 1:18). However, the angels see God in heaven and he was seen by the patriarchs and prophets. Moreover, he who sees me, sees the Father (Jn 14:19; Jn 1:14). The Holy Spirit appeared as a dove; and God can come to the saints in whatever way he chooses, but his nature remains hidden. Though we will not see God with our bodily eyes, a clean heart with God's grace prepares us to see him with our spiritual vision.

In the same year Augustine writes to Proba and her daughter-in-law Juliana, congratulating them when Juliana's daughter Demetrias became a consecrated virgin (L 150). It is certainly more glorious to be a virgin spouse of Christ than to be a worldly consul. For the virgin has a higher rank in heaven than any on earth. Augustine tells Proba and Juliana to pray for their daughter's vocation. May they enjoy in her what they gave up to have her as a child. May she have many imitators.

Augustine pens to Sapida, a consecrated virgin of Carthage (L 263). He kindly accepts the tunic which Sapida had woven for her deacon brother Timothy who had died suddenly before he could wear it. Another example of Augustine's kindness, taking after his most charitable mother. Timothy had admired Sapida's virgin calling so much. Augustine tries to console her by thoughts of heaven where her brother is now and where she will join him. "Tim loved and still loves Sapida."

Sorrow is proper at the time of bereavement, for Martha and Mary and Jesus cried when Lazarus died. Though God took Tim's soul, he will return it to his body. He does not need a tunic now for he is clothed in immortality.

On another occasion Augustine sent a note to Ecdicia, a married lady who foolishly took the vow of continence without her husband's permission, so he eventually turned to adultery to relieve his sexual tensions. Husband and wife owe each other mutual affection and the exchange of their bodies. Paul warns that spouses should not separate except for prayer and then only for a short while (1 Cor 7:1-5).

When Ecdicia first refused her husband intercourse, he went along with her dream for a while, but then fell back. "You should have given way to him all the more humbly and submissively in your domestic relationship," writes Augustine. Moreover, she had no right to dispose of family property without her husband's consent (Eph

5:23). Be like Sarah who obeyed her lord (Gn 18:12; 1 Pt 5-6). "You should have taken counsel together," deciding what property would be given away and what would be saved. Be subject to your husband as the head of the family for peace in the home.

Furthermore, a married woman should dress properly with decorum and not like a widow. Seek your husband's approval of your apparel. Even Queen Esther obeyed her pagan husband (Est 14:16). She should pray for her husband, apologize and promise. Moreover, he has the right to the custody of their son.

Writing to Fabiola in a distant city, Augustine notes that they can converse through their correspondence. For "if we know each other's thoughts we should be more together than if we were in one place, sitting in silence" (L 267).

Augustine exchanged notes with many other women, e.g. LL 92, 99, 124, 126, 127, 130, 131, 210. His letters are forms of personal instruction, answering questions and giving advice as best he can, but also learning from his correspondents.

Like many of the other Fathers, Augustine bases male/female relationships on the old Adam and Eve story and the Roman traditions including the *tutela mulierum* and the *infirmitas sexus*. In Augustine's day the Roman women were quite liberated, as we have seen. So the bishop is trying to uphold some of the older traditions which were going by the wayside.

We will discuss in a later book the salient place that Mary held in the Christian theology of the fourth and fifth century. This devotion seems to parallel the rising position of women in the Christian Roman society. Mary mystically combines the two main vocations of Christian women, namely virgin and mother. She is not the old sinning Eve who became subject to her husband, but rather the new Eve who cooperated with her son the new Adam in overcoming the sin of the garden pair. Moreover, in cancelling the sin, the new Adam and Eve made strides against the penalties, for in the kingdom there is to be no more submission of female to male.

The church, which we will speak of later, is ever the virgin spouse of Christ, and the mother of all Christians. Paul raised the Christian wife to a parallel with mother church, so her relationship with her husband is no longer that of Eve to Adam, but rather that of the church to the new Adam, Christ.

As we have seen, Augustine is a professional teacher, a rhetor, who instructs both men and women in his letters, sermons and counseling. In the following chapter we will see his philosophy and theology of education, of which we have already had some glimpses.

IX.
WHEREVER HE DISCOVERS TRUTH,
IT IS THE LORD'S

(Christian Doctrine 2, 18)

The Rhetor's Chair [1]

Augustine, exemplifying the syncretism necessary for good pedagogy, translated the ancient Christian traditions into the popular Neoplatonic philosophy of his day. Moreover, his Christian Neoplatonic school would dominate Western thought through the Middle Ages and into Reformation theology.

Augustine was one of the last great Roman teachers, flourishing just before the barbarian invasions. Safe in Africa, he was able to pursue his teaching, study and writing in his episcopal school at Hippo. His library of treatises, letters and sermons, edited by himself, has been preserved practically intact. He was one of the few teachers of all time who had the opportunity at the close of his career to get many of his notes in order, editing, commenting, giving reasons for and against former opinions in his *Retractations* (426-27).

Augustine was one of the last great rhetor-monk-bishops who include such giants as Basil, the two Gregories and John Chrysostom. As they were the beacons of Greek Christianity, Augustine's school would guide the West.

Augustine was many things: rhetor, philosopher, monk, bishop. But, first of all, he was a teacher, instructing in the African and Italian schools from 373 to 386. Like many of his Christian predecessors and contemporaries, he quit his rhetor's chair at his conversion. However, Augustine did not give up his teaching, but rather switched from the *paideia* (teaching) of Cicero to that of Jesus Christ, at the same time taking along his rhetorical methodology.

Born in Thagaste in 354, Augustine studied in nearby Madaura (365-69) and then pursued the rhetorical course at Carthage (370-73).

---

1. This chapter first appeared in *The School of Jesus* (New York: Alba House, 1972).

While there he discovered Cicero's philosophy as taught in his Hortensius.[1] Whereas rhetoric stressed method and elocution, philosophy points more to what is spoken.

After teaching grammar for a year at Thagaste, Augustine returned to Carthage as a rhetor. But in 383 he set sail for Rome, a more attractive educational center.

> The greatest and almost the sole reason was because I had heard that young men studied there in a more peaceful way and were kept by the restraints of a better order and discipline. They were not allowed to rush insolently and at random into the classroom of a teacher with whom they were not enrolled, nor were they let in at all unless he gave permission. (*Confessions* 5, 8)

Recent Roman law ensured the proper conduct of students. For example, when they arrived at Rome, they had to go immediately to the tax assessor with their birth certificate and a letter of recommendation. Also they must indicate in what profession they wish to study.

> In the third place, the office of tax assessment shall carefully investigate the life of the students at their lodging places to see that they actually do bestow their time on the studies which they assert that they are pursuing. These same officials shall warn the students that they shall severally conduct themselves in their assemblies as persons should who consider it their duty to avoid a disgraceful and scandalous reputation and bad associations, all of which we consider as the next worse thing to actual criminality. Nor shall the students attend shows too frequently nor commonly take part in unseasonable carousals. We further grant you as prefect the authority that, if any student in the city should fail to conduct himself as the dignity of a liberal education demands, he shall be publicly flogged, immediately put on board a boat, expelled from the city and returned home. (C.Th.14, 9, 1) (March 12, 370)[2]

If they were not finished with their studies by their twentieth year, they were to be shipped back home forthwith.

Augustine was glad to get rid of the wild Carthaginian boys who rushed in and out of classrooms, disrupting discipline. At Rome he set up his rhetorical school in his home, gathering students with whom he hoped to build a reputation. However, the Roman students, though

---

1. *Confessions*, 3, 4.
2. *The Theodosian Code*, tr., C. Pharr (Princeton University Press, 1952), 414.

more orderly, were also more slippery, transferring from one teacher to another in order to avoid paying tuition.

As soon as a rhetor's chair opened up at Milan, Augustine applied for it. There he met Bishop Ambrose who introduced him to the joys of Neoplatonism. However, he soon experienced a conversion (386), abandoning his profession to seek the peace and contemplation of a friend's villa at Cassiciacum. "Some of your servants, my brothers, may say that I sinned in this matter, in that, with a heart now completely in your service, I allowed myself to sit for a single hour in that chair of lies" (*Confessions* 9, 2). Augustine's ill health was another factor in his resignation.

Philosophical School at Cassiciacum

There were numerous examples of Christian converts leaving their rhetors' chairs. Reborn in baptism, they left their past lives entirely behind. Relinquishing the pagan classics, their new *paideia* was that of Christ. To his dying day Augustine was destined to be a magister. So when he retired to Cassiciacum for a few months' rest, he started a philosophical school there, teaching in the popular dialogue form, going back to ancient times. Besides his mother Monica, his son Adeodatus, his Brother Navigius, friends Alypius and Evodius, there were two young boys sent by their parents for instruction.

These halcyon scholastic days Augustine called, "*Christianae vitae otium*" (*Retractations* 1, 1). Augustine's delight in these friendly dialogues may be found in his discussions *On the Happy Life*. Whether the conversations are real or merely literary forms, they probably have some basis in his teaching methodology. Moreover, these lively exchanges were appreciated by both teacher and students. "You have truly contributed so much to our discussion that I cannot deny that I have been sated by my own guests" (*On the Happy Life* 36).

Augustine always had the heart of a teacher. For example, he never talked down to his students or lectured them, but respected their persons, loved them — the essence of Greek *paiderastia*. The Cassiciacum dialogues bring this out. Augustine's enthusiasm and expectancy constantly pop up with both students and teacher learning from each other. A certain amount of camaraderie and light-hearted kidding were the order of the day. As an experienced teacher, Augustine did not rush through the matter, but let the dialogue follow the students' pace, repeating the matter whenever a slower one might ask a question.

As Howie points out, the Cassiciacum dialogues illustrate well

Augustine's active teaching method.[1] Rather than lectures, they are explorations into a problem whether it be the happy life, or the principle of order. By and large they are what moderns would call group learning experiences. Anyone who hopes for orderly progress and fixed conclusions will be disappointed. Later dialogues *On Music, Greatness of the Soul* and *The Teacher* are more stilted.

Although at times the discussion may seem to be directionless, Augustine would intervene when it got too far off the track.[2] After a long prelude by their mentor, the students take over the conversation. Then when he feels that they have gone far enough, Augustine gives a concluding exposition. Having wandered hither and yon, his pupils are now willing to listen to directions.

In promoting the dialogues, Augustine recognizes a basic pedagogical principle, namely, one really teaches oneself with God's help. He used the Socratic question and answer method to bring out the best in his protégés, at the same time taking great care not to embarrass them.

Since, on the one hand, truth cannot be better pursued than by question and answer, and since, on the other hand, hardly anyone can be found who is not ashamed to be defeated in an argument, with the result that it almost always happens that a subject for discussion which is well begun is driven out of mind by the unruly noise of self-opinion, accompanied also by wounded feelings which are usually concealed but at times evident — for these reasons, it was my pleasure to seek the truth with God's help in peace and propriety by questioning and answering myself.[3]

Augustine prided himself on the progress of his students, writing their parents a good report when they had made some advance.[4]

In the Cassiciacum seminar spontaneity is of the essence. Augustine senses when his companions are eager to tackle some relevant problem of the day. And sometimes the question they start out with is not the same one they end up with. For example, they might begin with an inquiry into the meaning of happiness. But happiness is searching for the truth. What is truth?

Augustine's Cassiciacum school did not have regular classes, but rather lively discussions after meals or when the farm chores were finished. In fair weather they went out into the flowery meadow and

---

1. *Educational Theory and Practice in Augustine* (London: Routledge and Kegan Paul, 1969), 164.

2. *Against the Academics* 1, 4.

3. *Soliloquies* 2, 7.

4. *Against the Academics* 1, 4.

sat underneath a spreading oak tree. If it started to rain, they repaired to the baths to continue their conversation. Often they talked late into the night, and, on at least one occasion, in the dormitory.[1]

Augustine had an insatiable inquiring mind, never resting until he found the cause of something. And he instilled this same curiosity in his students. He was a father to them, delighting in their growth toward maturity.

I could not restrain my joy in seeing this young man (Trygetius), the son of a very dear friend, becoming my son also; and still more in seeing him growing and developing into a friend, when I had despaired of being able to cultivate in him a taste even for the ordinary study of literature.[2]

After his conversion, Augustine took his little group of Servants of God back to his family place at Thagaste, where they continued their enthusiastic discussions.

Let us now look at several works which Augustine wrote specifically about Christian education, including *The Teacher* (389), *First Catechetical Instruction* (405), and *Christian Doctrine* (397, 426).

Christ, The Master

In *The Teacher,* probably dedicated to Adeodatus who had just died at the young age of sixteen, the central theme repeats the basic message of both Jewish and Christian revelation—here with Platonic over-tones—namely, that God alone is our teacher. Here, of course, he teaches through his Son, Jesus Christ, who throughout all of Christian tradition has been *The Teacher*, with all subsequent instructors subordinate to the Master.

The Teacher is a dialogue between Augustine and Adeodatus, starting out to find the purpose of speaking—to teach or to remind (1, 1). Then Augustine draws an important distinction between realities and words. The supreme Teacher taught his disciples by means of words and signs (1, 2). And the realities are more important than the signs. "For whatever exists for the sake of something else must be inferior to that for whose sake it exists" (9, 25). Of course, signs are an essential part of teaching, though not necessarily verbal signs. Thus

1. *On Order* 1, 8.
2. *Ibid.,* 1, 6.

one can also guide by one's actions. And, indeed, Jesus taught both ways, by word and example.

However, the signs themselves do not teach, but rather lead the way to learning the truth. For when a sign is presented to me, if it finds me ignorant of the reality of which it is the sign, it cannot teach me anything. But if it finds me knowing the reality, what do I learn by means of the sign? (10, 33) (A).

Not by external words do we learn, but by the internal Teacher, Christ. The internal light here is a popular Platonic theme in Augustine, the divine light illuminating the unchangeable truths. Just as the sun aids the human eye to see by shining on its object, so the interior light brightens the object of the mind, the eye of the soul.[1] Of course, John, also Greek influenced, had called Jesus the light (1:4-5).

> Regarding, however, all those things which we understand, it is not a speaker who utters sounds exteriorly whom we consult, but it is the truth that presides within, over the mind itself, though it may have been the words that prompted us to make such consultation. (11, 38)

But if Christ, the Teacher, instructs us internally, does not this make the external teacher superfluous? Augustine platonically explains teaching as primarily reminding. Most teachers do not give their own thoughts to their students, but rather transmit branches of learning, rhetoric, mathematics, etc.

> When the teachers have explained, by means of words, all those subjects which they profess to teach, and even the science of virtue and of wisdom, then those who are called pupils consider within themselves whether what has been said is true. This they do by gazing attentively at that interior truth, so far as they are able. (14)

Are pupils, then, self-taught? Not really, for they are taught internally by the divine light. But why do they call their external prompter, teacher? Because there is such a short interval between the external and internal teaching. "He himself will teach us, who has counseled us through the instrumentality of human beings – by means of signs, and externally – to turn to him internally and be instructed" (14).

---

1. *The Trinity* 12, 15.

First Catechetical Instruction

It was Augustine's teaching and writing ability, along with his piety, which attracted the people of Hippo to choose him first as presbyter and then as bishop. As a teacher-bishop Augustine is concerned primarily with the instruction of catechumens. Since Christianity is basically *paideia*, from the beginning it had been necessary to teach the newcomers the way of Christ. Moreover, since it is a book religion, like its mother Judaism, the sacred books had to be explained. Often the former religions of the catechumens whether pagan or Jewish are shown in the apologetic manner to be inferior. Next the convert is taught his existential place in the world by a brief sketch of salvation history from Adam up to Christ who initiated the final stage into which the new Christian is now entering.

There are four classes of people on the road to Christianity: *accedentes*, candidates for admission to the catechumenate; catechumens; *competentes*, catechumens approved for baptism at the Easter Vigil; *neophyti*, the newly baptized, whose instruction continued through the Easter octave. The great episcopal catecheses of Gregory, Cyril, Ambrose, Theodore of Mopsuestia are addressed to the last two groups, while the deacons instruct the beginners.

In fact, it is to deacon Deogratias of Carthage that Augustine sends his instructions on the catechizing of the *accedentes* (405). Augustine limits this to one instruction, including a brief narration of salvation history and an exhortation to the Christian moral life, based on the two great commandments.

Besides two sample catecheses, Augustine gives some practical hints for successful instruction, no doubt garnered from his long years as a pedagogue. This work on catechetics along with its companion volume on *Christian Doctrine* (397, 426), a textbook of homiletics, would serve as a basis of monastic education, led by outstanding teachers such as Cassiodorus, Isadore, Bede, Alquin and Rabanus Maurus.

The catechesis itself should sketch briefly an outline of salvation history, including the Old Testament, the coming of Christ as a manifestation of God's love down to the present stage of church history. At the same time, the candidate should be questioned concerning his or her motives for joining the church (3-6), followed by the moral exhortation underlining certain temptations open to the catechumens. For example, they should avoid non-believers and sinners such as drunkards, adulterers and the like (7).

All students should be treated alike, but according to their educational background. Since some come already skilled in the scriptures, they should not be bored by repetition. Do not be afraid to build on their classical backgrounds, at the same time weaning them away from any heretical teachings they may have read.

Students from the grammar and rhetorical schools should be trained in humility and shown that the simple doctrines of scriptures are not to be taken literally, but rather explored for their hidden spiritual meanings.

> For it is most useful for these men to know that the meaning is to be regarded as superior to words, just as the spirit is to be preferred to the body. And from this, too, it follows that they ought to prefer to hear true rather than eloquent discourses, just as they ought to prefer to have wise rather than handsome friends. (9) (A)

Moreover, these wise fellows should not make fun of the imperfect diction of often poorly educated ministers of the church, a common problem in the days of Augustine.

Augustine encourages Deogratias who is depressed and bored at his thankless task. Catechists often suffer from the occupational hazard of spiritual torpor, which leaves them down in the dumps and weary of mind. Augustine analyzes one cause.

> Just because the subjects that the candidates have to be taught are now so familiar to us and no longer necessary for our progress, it irks us to return to them so often. And our mind, as having outgrown them, no longer moves with any pleasure in such well-trodden and, as it were, childish paths. Moreover, a hearer who remains unmoved makes the speaker weary. (10)

Sometimes the catechist is speaking over the pupil's head and must slow down, lowering his sights till he reaches the level of intelligence of his listeners. Language is a problem, for often the words of the catechist do not adequately express the ineffable mysteries, and sometimes mistakes are made. At other times the listener thinks the Christian doctrine harsh. In all of these, clarifications should be made from both reason and authority (11).

The boredom which settles over both pupils and teacher may be healed by a sympathetic love for the students and a sincere attempt to see the ancient and repetitious truths anew through the fresh eyes of the learner.

> Again, if it is distasteful for us to be repeating over and over things that are familiar and suitable for little children, let us suit ourselves to them with a brother's, a father's and a mother's love,

and when we are linked to them thus in heart these things will seem new even to us. For so great is the power of sympathy, that when people are affected by us as we speak and we by them as they learn, we dwell each in the other and thus both they, as it were, speak in us what they hear, while we, after a fashion, learn in them what we teach. (12)

The interpenetration of teacher and student in the learning process has rarely been better expressed.

There are other causes of apathy among the students. One is shyness. "We must drive out by gentle encouragement his excessive timidity, which hinders him from expressing his opinion. We must temper his shyness by introducing the idea of brotherly fellowship" (13). Judicious questioning may bolster his confidence.

Sometimes the candidate is just physically tired out from the day's labors or from the previous night on the town, or just fatigued from standing and listening to a droning catechist, yearning for the end of class. Wake him up by saying something personal. Offer him a seat, make him comfortable.

A final word of advice concerns the type of audience, whether in private or in public, few or many, learned or unlearned, city slickers or country bumpkins, or mixed. Of course, the well-educated upper classes are more pleasing to teach. In general, the candidates should be grouped according to their abilities.

Augustine concluded his work on catechetics with a model discourse, both in long and short form with its brief narrative of salvation history and its moral exhortation based on the decalogue and the two great commandments.

Christian Doctrine

The companion volume to Augustine's *First Catechetical Instruction* is his *Christian Doctrine* (397, 426). In books one and two he writes of sacred and profane subjects necessary as preparation for reading and interpreting the Bible including: God, the Trinity, wisdom, Christ, church, resurrection, brotherly love, the relationship between God and man, scripture and its interpretation; the nature of signs and writing, steps to wisdom, the canon of scriptures, the languages of scripture and their translations.

Augustine's attitude toward pagan writers mirrors his contemporaries. Use what is useful, discard what is not. "Every good and true Christian should understand that wherever he discovers truth, it is the Lord's" (2, 18). Some sciences are dangerous and superstitious, for example, astrology. On the other hand, many branches of secular learning aid us in our study of sacred scripture, namely: history; the science of animals, plants and the stars; mechanical arts (2, 30). Dialectics (including conclusions, definitions and divisions) and rhetoric are also useful, not to mention mathematics. However, all these should be studied in moderation (2, 39).

> God's truth also may be found among the pagans.
> If those who are called philosophers, especially the Platonists, have said things by chance that are truthful and comfortable to our faith we must not only have no fear of them, but even appropriate them from our own use from those who are, in a sense, their illegal possessors. (2, 40)

However, pagan knowledge, no matter how high, is inferior to the scriptures (2, 42).

The third book of *Christian Doctrine* is devoted to hermeneutics, explaining the various senses of scripture and also including the seven rules of Tyconius for unlocking the secrets of the Bible. The fourth book is a manual of homiletics, giving practical suggestions to the Christian teacher, based on Cicero and Quintilian's rhetorical principles.

Certainly the Christian teacher should make use of eloquence. "Why, then, do not the good zealously procure it (eloquence) that it may serve the truth, if the wicked, in order to gain unjustifiable and groundless errors apply it to the advantage of injustice and error?" (4, 2).

If his listeners are ignorant, the Christian teacher must instruct them. If, on the other hand, they are already knowledgeable, but indifferent — he must inspire them. "In that case, entreaty and reproof, exhortation and rebuke, and all other means designed to rouse hearts, are indispensable" (4, 4). However, both wisdom and eloquence are needed, for it is not enough to be an expert orator if one has nothing to say.

For the sake of clarity, difficult passages of scripture should be avoided in public. The teacher should, as far as possible, speak in the language of his students, though his diction may be colloquial and even incorrect.

> Good teachers have, or ought to have, such great care in teaching that, where a word cannot be pure Latin without being obscure, they should use it according to idiomatic usage, if it avoids

ambiguity and obscurity. They should employ it not as it is used by the learned, but rather as the unlearned usually express it. (4, 10)

Augustine gives the example of *os* which can mean either mouth or bone, confusing the simple people. Why not use *ossum* for bone whose plural is *ossa*? Here we have the very foundation of good teaching, communication and relevance. Both teacher and student must speak the same language. "What benefit is a purity of speech which the understanding of the hearer does not follow, since there is no reason at all for speaking, if those for whose enlightenment we are speaking do not understand what we are saying" (4, 10).

Augustine especially warns against an ominous silence during class or a sermon. Since a crowd that wants to learn shows this by its movement, Augustine encourages applause or other reactions to his teachings. If someone has his speech all memorized, he cannot go over matters again in order to call attention to a particular point that needs special emphasis. Room must be left for spontaneity.

Quoting Cicero, Augustine maintains that it is not enough to teach, but one must also please and persuade.[1] The first depends on what we say, while the second and third rely on how we say it. "Just as he is pleased if you speak attractively, so he is moved if he finds pleasure in what you promise, dreads what you threaten, hates what you condemn, etc." (4, 12).

Moreover, the teacher should vary the form of his presentation. For example, if the grand style is pursued too long, it will make people edgy. So it is best to alternate the grand and subdued styles like the waves of the ocean. The introduction should always be moderate, while knotty problems are discussed in a more laid back manner. In a word, moderation pleases, while the grand manner persuades (4, 23).

But no matter what style the teacher uses, his life should mirror his words. It is possible to benefit some by preaching alone. However, if one practices what he says, there will be a much greater effect.

We have seen several of Augustine's works on Christian education. But some of his keenest hints may be found in other treatises. For example, *The Trinity* (399-416). In order to attempt to bring this profound mystery home to his listeners, he illustrates it with human triads, for we are made in the image of the triune God. Some examples: lover, loved and love (8, 10); mind, knowledge and love (9, 4); memory, intellect and will (14).

Like Plato, Augustine places the stress on love and memory in his theory of knowledge. Some slight understanding is required first to stimulate a love of learning. And the more a thing is known, but not

1. *On Oratory* 2, 27.

fully known, the more the mind desires to know the rest (10, 1). The scholar is driven on in his desire for the splendor of knowledge. "The splendor of such knowledge is already seen in his thoughts, and is loved by him as something known. And it is so seen and so arouses the zeal of learners that they are spurred into activity on account of it" (10, 1). Something that they know only in theory such as a foreign language, they desire to master also in practice.

Despair is the bane of all learning, for it crushes desire. Subjects are studied more eagerly when people do not despair of being able to grasp them. When a man has not the hope of being able to attain his end, he either loves the object in a lukewarm manner or does not love it at all, however valuable he may see it to be. (10, 1)

The implications for a teacher are clear. He must start with what the student already knows and instill in him or her a desire to know what they do not yet know with the enthusiasm of the teacher carrying the students over discouragement and despair, while urging them on to greater heights.

Augustine talks about his teaching mission to his young protégée Florentina, who has asked for his help (L 266). He had earlier corresponded with Florentina's mother. "I owe to the extent of my ability as a free service to your admirable study and that of all like you." Augustine does not want to close the "door of assurance" against her, or in any way condescend.

Florentina should ask any question she wants to and Augustine will try to answer in the best way that he can. Sometimes she spurs him to study up on something that he does not know. So they mutually stimulate each other in their learning.

Augustine does not consider himself a finished master, but as one needing to be perfected along with his students. "Excellent lady, daughter deservedly honored and cherished in Christ, I am more anxious for you to be learned than to be in need of my learning."

The teacher has to constantly guard against pride. Augustine delights in Florentina's progress so that eventually she will need no human teacher. Even Paul sensed his own inadequacy as a pedagogue (2 Cor 12:7). For there is only one master, Jesus Christ (Mt 23:8, 10). While Paul may plant and water, it is God who gives the increase (1 Cor 3:7).

Granted that Augustine's instructions may be helpful to Florentina, the interior Master will reveal to her heart that it is God himself who stimulates her growth.

In conclusion, then, we have seen something of Augustine the teacher. Though called reluctantly to administer the church of Hippo, Augustine was first, last and always a teacher. Trained in the rhetoric of Cicero and Quintilian, he taught first at Carthage, then at Rome and Milan.

At Cassiciacum he began his career as a Christian teacher, starting with philosophical dialogues here and at Thagaste and continuing through his catecheses and homilies at Hippo. Truly after Jesus and Paul, Augustine is the teacher of the West and his educational theories, especially as seen in his *First Catechetical Instruction* and his *Christian Doctrine,* were foundations of Western monastic education and indirectly influenced the medieval universities.

Augustine is both a teacher in the church and a teacher of the church, concerned with the instruction of beginners and explaining the divine mysteries to his varied flock. One of Augustine's favorite topics is social justice, or the sharing of our earthly goods with the less fortunate. We will see more of this in the following chapter.

X.

THE RICH AND POOR ARE EQUAL IN BIRTH AND DEATH

(Sermon 61)

Christian and Roman Social Justice

Practically all cultures tell stories of the primordial halcyon times when all was right with the world with no greed, lust or injustice. For all were equal and all goods held in common.

In more advanced peoples the monastic tradition tried to keep this ideal alive with the communism of a large extended family. Hindus, Buddhists, Jews and Christians were attracted to this way of life.[1] The Jewish rabbinical *haburah* (fellowship) influenced early Christianity which tried the common way in the beginning but soon found it impractical in a property-oriented Roman empire (Rom 10:12, AA 2, 44).

Jesus counseled the rich young man to sell all, give to the poor and join his *haburah* (fellowship), the shibboleth of Christian monasticism (Mk 10:17, Mt 19:16, Lk 18:18). Yet when the wealthy youth rejected the Master's offer, Jesus still loved him. No doubt he was a good steward of God's largess, though not a total renunciator.

Jesus said that though the poor have little of this world's goods, they will share in Paradise where all are equal (Lk 16:19, 31). Both Jesus and Paul (Lk 19:1; 2 Cor 8:14) praise those who share their possessions with the poor.

Christianity, like Pharisaism, appealed to the little people, the disenfranchised. Church Fathers continued the Judaeo-Christian ideal of stewardship rather than the encouragement to the ownership of private property in Roman law. For God is the real owner of all. Moreover, the obligation to share our superfluities is in justice not in charity.

---

1. See J. Mohler, *The Heresy of Monasticism* (New York: Alba House, 1971).

Basil said that those who claim an absolute right to private property are really atheists for they deny the divine ownership of the world.[1] Basil imitated the Coptic monks in the common life of his monastery.

Even the sophisticated Romans harked back to the paradisal times of Saturn when all was held in common and justice reigned. Each winter they commemorated these happy days in their Saturnalia when slaves ruled their masters, and business and school were recessed for reveling and joy.

Farmers were seen as the descendants of King Saturn, the Sower. However, by Varro's time (1 C., BC) the wealthy patricians were gathering up the small family farms into huge estates. Virgil hopes for a return to the age of Saturn under Augustus when peace will reign and the land will be free.[2] For before Jove all things were held in common. And the Romans never lost their nostalgia for the golden age of Saturn, even though the patricians controlled the land, charging high rent or service to the plebians who were working the soil.

Though originally the land was not part of the *res mancipi,* it was included as such in the Twelve Tables (450, BC). As absentee ownership of the land grew, many of the exploited tenants fled to the city where they swelled the ranks of the unemployed. Many slaves added to the wealth of the landowners until at the time of Augustus the ratio had risen to 3/5, slave/free.

The ownership of private property (*dominium*) appeared at the end of the Republic. *Dominium* gave the *pater familias* complete control over all his possessions including family, slaves and property. However it was not absolute, for the common good takes precedence. And the Roman emperors such as Diocletian chastised the greedy who undermined the economy by their profiteering and speculation. Gradually the patricians lost power to the *Equites* whose nobility was based on wealth or office.

The Stoics, popular Roman philosophers who influenced Christianity, taught the brotherhood and sisterhood of the human race, stressing the sharing rather than the hoarding of wealth. Basically Stoic doctrine seems to reflect the early myths when all was held in common and there were no rich or poor.

The idea was to make the little men or women important. Orates and Zeno said that all are brothers and sisters without distinction and united in love.[3] Seneca, first century Stoic, valued his slaves not for what they did for him, but rather for who they were in themselves. What is important is not what we possess, but who we are, that is,

---

1. *On Luke,* "*Destruam* . . ." 7.
2. *Eclogue* 4, 17; *Aeneid* 6, 790-800.
3. *The Stoic Philosophy of Seneca* (Garden City: Doubleday, 1958), 19.

virtuous, honorable and reasonable (L 76). The only good is that which makes the soul better.

Seneca argues that if we have money and power which the gods do not possess, we should be happier than they are. Actually earthly wealth is a burden because it is necessarily transitory. For we are born and die poor. Though the Stoic may appear poor on the outside, within he is rich in virtue. The Stoics influenced the Neoplatonists, the Christian monks and fathers, for example, Ambrose and Augustine.

Ambrose: Store It in the Hearts of the Poor

When he was chosen bishop of Milan, Ambrose gave his wealth to the needy. And as bishop he was open to all classes of people from the emperor down to the poorest beggar.

The large Roman landholders had increased their holdings at the expense of the small family farm, as we have seen. So when the empire became Christian, the bishops defended the poor from exploitation by excommunicating the offenders, or through civil power, as well.

Bishop Ambrose wrote his work on Naboth the Jezreelite against the social evils of the time, chastising the greedy and luxury-loving rich who were robbing the poor. Ambrose quoted from the Bible, Basil and classical authors to back up his case.[1]

Who was Naboth? A farmer of Jezreel who was murdered in a plot by Jezebel so that her husband, King Ahab of Israel, might acquire Naboth's land, which he did not want to sell. The prophet Elijah condemned the house of Ahab for their crime. For it was an ancient Israelite custom that land should remain in the family and not be absorbed into huge estates.

Ambrose notes (1) that times have not changed. For the rich of his day still covet the goods of others, driving off the poor in order to take over their acres — modern Ahabs and Naboths. Though the earth was made for all to enjoy, the rich claim exclusive right to the soil. Nature, who begets all poor, does not know the rich. Naked we are born and naked we die. So all are the same in the cemetery.

Ambrose comments that the rich are really poor, for the more they have, the more they want (2). Their avarice is enkindled by gain. Who is really poor? "He who is content with his own or who covets another's property?"

---

1. *S. Ambrosii de Nabuthe,* M. McGuire, ed. and tr. (Washington: Catholic University Press), 11. Next few quotes are from here.

He continues, "You believe it your loss, whatever is another's." The world was created for the use of all mankind. Yet the few rich are trying to appropriate it for themselves. Not only the earth, but also the sky, air and seas are claimed (3).

How many poor die, working their hearts out for the rich? "The whole people groan, yet you alone, O rich man, are not moved" (5). What good are riches if they do not free us from death? For rich and poor alike have the same fate (6).

The rich hold onto their barns full of grain, waiting for the price to go up. Yet meanwhile they lose the enjoyment of its benefits and the hungry poor suffer even more (7). The miser worries that his large harvests will mean low prices. "For abundance belongs to all, while scarcity is lucrative to the miser alone." Why make evils from goods? Rather we should make goods from evils. If we know how to use them, they are goods. If not, they are evils.

They are goods, if we give to the poor and needy. "Store it in the hearts of the poor." The spiritual farmer sows what will bring him or her profit, that is, sowing in the hearts of widows. If the earth returns our planting with interest, how much more will our mercy return to us?

Some are always counting their gold and silver. "How much better would it be, were you a generous distributor rather than an anxious custodian." While our money stays here below, our charity accompanies us to heaven (8).

"Mercy, sown on earth, germinates in heaven, is transplanted in the poor man and grows with God" (12). "Not from your own do you bestow on the poor, but you return what is really theirs. For what has been given in common for all, you appropriate to yourself alone."

Ambrose proceeds more vehemently, "You rich clothe your very walls, while you strip men of their clothes," neglecting the naked who beg before your very door. Though the beggar shivers without a warm wool cloak, the rich worry about the travertine marble they have ordered to cover their floors (13).

While a hungry man needs bread, the horse of the rich man chomps on a golden bridle. "While people starve, the barns of the wealthy are locked up. Only one jewel from his ring could save the whole people."

Be a custodian, not a master of your wealth, says Ambrose, since you are its servant, not its lord (14). For where our heart is, our treasure is. Sell gold and buy salvation. "Possessions ought to belong to the possessor," and not vice versa. Thus one who does not give to the poor "is servant of his wealth, not its master" (15).

Speaking of the duties of the clergy, Ambrose notes that *officium* (duty, service, business, office) is derived from *efficere* (to effect).

"You should do only those things which injure (*officiant*) no one, but benefit all."[1]

Greed should have no place in the life of the clergy (1 Tim 3:2-10) (1, 50). Moreover, the clerics should not even be engaged in business (1, 36). "Be entangled not in the things of this life, for you are fighting for God" (1 Tim 2:4). The soldiers of the emperor cannot sue, own a business or engage in retailing. So much more so should he who fights for Christ "keep from every kind of business, being satisfied with the produce of his own little bit of land, if he has it."

If not, let him be satisfied with his small wage (Ps 37), enjoying true rest and peace of mind, "which is not excited by the desire of gain, nor tormented by the fear of want." So the clergy should lead their flocks by the example of their own penury and their personal battle against greed.

Ambrose divides *officium* into two parts: ordinary and perfect (1, 11). The first consists of the ten commandments (Mt 19:17-19), while perfection means selling all, giving to the poor and following Christ (Mt 19:20-21).

The Greeks called perfection *katorthoma,* by which all things are put right. Our mercy makes us perfect because it imitates the Father, who is kind to the poor, "who are sharers in common with you in the produce of nature, which brings forth the fruits of the earth for the use of all." Give freely to your poor brother, for your silver gives him life and your money is his only possession.

"He gives more to you than you to him, since he is your debtor in regard to your salvation," bringing you righteousness, and the friendship of the saints and heaven (Jb 29:15-16). The Lord also becomes his debtor, for his mercy will be rewarded on the last day.

In the common view justice does not injure except in retaliation. But the gospels contradict, treating public property as public and private as private. However, although nature gives all things in common, greed wants to take everything.

In his discussion of creation Ambrose notes that the fish of the sea divide up the waters so all have sufficient space.[2] However, men tend to hog the land, taking on new estates, households and even the sea.

Though we may have a fine home, flocks and other wealth, we should not forget from whom all these good things come and that they are, indeed, transitory gifts. Look in the grave and see who is rich or poor, weak or powerful there (6, 8).

Though the poor may lack money, they need not be short on grace. "Rich and poor alike enjoy the splendid ornaments of the universe."

---

1. *De Officiis* 1, 8 (N). Next few quotes are from here.
2. *Hexaemeron* 5, 10.

While the rich may delight in their fancy frescoed ceilings, the poor have the beautiful heavens to admire.

The poor should not envy the rich, for they only want more. Besides, earthly goods are a poor investment for heaven. The poor man saves up his interest, while the wealthy one squanders it. We have enough when we have a sufficiency of this world's goods; for a rich person tends to burden his mind. However, the wise one only asks for what is necessary and adequate.

In Ambrose's and patristic tradition the right to own is not based on civil law, but rather due to God's dominion and human stewardship. So our right to ownership is not absolute, but rather dependent on the rights and needs of others. Roman law agrees.

We are all born needy and die needy. It is between birth and death that some acquire more than others either through inheritance or through acquisitions in business or crime. We violate nature, as the Stoics teach, if what was given to all, namely, land, sea, air, forests, etc. is appropriated by a few.

Augustine: Your Property is Mine

Augustine felt the same way as Ambrose and other Fathers and even some Roman emperors and satirists, namely, that in the perfect order there should not be rich and poor. We have seen Augustine's longing for the ideal of the gospels and Antony, namely, selling, giving to the poor and following Christ often in some form of common life.

Wealth should be a means to an end to help us toward eternal life and not to be enjoyed in itself, for only God can be loved in himself.

North Africa in the fifth century was largely agricultural. After the defeat of Carthage in 146 B.C., the land was taken over by Rome but eventually sold to large investors who paid taxes to the state. Thus grew vast latifundia with a few wealthy absentee landowners controlling their estates which were farmed by slaves or tenants to produce grain to feed the empire.

Augustine contrasts the temporal and eternal laws.[1] Under the temporal law we love worldly things: honor, power, pleasure, beauty which are ephemeral, while the eternal law says to turn from finite things to the infinite.

What does the temporal law say? Though people may be inordinately attached to worldly goods, they "should possess them by virtue of

---

1. *Free Choice* 1, 15.

that right which preserves peace and human society, so far as is possible in such affairs." Moreover, the Roman law can confiscate goods, if ill used.

> As long as they fear to lose these goods, they practice a kind of moderation in their use, capable of holding together a society that can be formed from men of this stamp. The law does not punish the sin committed by loving these things, but rather the crime of taking them from others unjustly.

Captivated by our love of temporal goods, we become subject to them, so that the means become our goal and true good. When they are used rightly, we see that they are not true goods for they do not make us good. And if we are not attached to them, we possess and control them, ready to leave them if necessary.

Frui et Uti

We have seen the contrast of *frui* and *uti*, enjoyment and use, in Augustine's discussion of human love.[1] We should only enjoy God as our final and absolute good. All creatures, including human beings, should be used to help us reach our final enjoyment of God.

Some things are to be enjoyed, others to be used, still others to be used and enjoyed.[2] The used things help us to attain the things that make us happy. However, if we enjoy the things to be used, we are drawn away from the final perfect good, God.

If we love another human being for his or her own sake, we enjoy him or her. But if we love the other for God's sake, we use him or her to help us attain eternal life. We should also love ourselves for God's sake.

Alms given to the righteous poor are the cornerstone of justice. While some seek alms for themselves, alms should seek out the righteous.[3]

> You will never do this, unless you have somewhat set aside from your substance, each what pleases him, according to the needs of his family as a sort of debt to be paid to the treasury.

---

1. Chapter V.
2. *Christian Doctrine* 1, 3.
3. On Psalm 146, 13.

Out of some fixed sum either from your yearly profits or daily gains. One tenth is too small for we should exceed the generosity of the Pharisees.

Two Cities

Though Augustine's two cities are incompatible, they coexist. So citizens of the heavenly city live with others, but not like them. The worldly see earthly goods as things to be enjoyed in themselves and not to be used as means to the true good, God.

God gave us gifts for our earthly health, security and fellowship: light, speech, air, water and all other things necessary to feed, clothe, heal and beautify our bodies. "He who uses these goods properly will receive abundant and better goods—immortal peace, enjoying God and his neighbor in God in eternal life." However, if these gifts are misused, he will lose them here and also lose eternal life.

While the earthly city uses temporal goods to reach earthly peace, in the heavenly city they are used to attain eternal rest (19, 14).

To promote right order we should harm no one and help whomever we can. The religious person serves those whom he rules not out of domination, but from duty, not out of pride, but because of paternal solicitude.

God gave man dominion over fish, birds, cattle, etc. (19, 15). "God wanted rational man, made to his image, to have no dominion except over irrational nature." Thus in olden times holy men were shepherds rather than rulers. So it was not God's original plan to subjugate human beings to each other. Rather this is a result of sin, e.g., Noe's son. Otherwise there is little mention of servants in the Old Testament. "Servant is a name that is not natural, but rather one that is deserved because of sin."

Servus means to be saved, because slaves were spared from death by their captors. However, without sin there would be no slavery. For sinners are slaves to their sins (Jn 8:34, 2 Pt 2:19). In this sense wicked masters are also slaves. While in the present order some were subject to others, "when their nature was as God created it, no man was a slave either to man or to sin."

Paul lived in the Roman empire when slavery was a part of everyday life. So he told the slaves to obey their masters (Eph 6:5-7). If there is no chance for manumission, they should make their slavery into freedom by serving in love, loyalty and tranquility until justice comes once again to the world. "And every human sovereignty and power is done away with so that God may be all in all."

Many Roman Christians had slaves, but they had the same status as children, under the care of the *pater familias* who wanted eternal life for his whole house (19, 16). Discipline is necessary for peace in the home and in society.

Good Christians should use their material and temporal goods in the spirit of pilgrims to help ease the burden of the body (19, 17).

While the earthly city seeks an earthly peace, the heavenly metropolis must also use this same harmony and so should obey the civil laws. Thus there is a common cause between the two cities in what concerns our human living.

Imagine two people, each a part of a city or a kingdom (4, 3). While one is poor or in moderate circumstances, the other one is wealthy. And while the rich person is constantly haunted by fear and greed, piling up money and worries, the modest one is content and peaceful in good conscience. Who has the better life?

What is the basis of ownership, Augustine asks. "Is it not a human right?"[1] By divine right the earth and its fullness is the Lord's. Poor and rich God made out of the same clay and God's earth supports both. Human rights say, "This is mine!" specified by the laws of the emperors.

What about usury, which is forbidden by the law? Is this not worse than stealing from the rich? However, the civil courts do not demand restitution to the poor.

Those who rejoice in their wealth, but use it unjustly, "are really in possession of other's property. He who uses his wealth badly possesses it wrongfully. And wrongful possession means that it is another's property." See how many owe restitution.

In this life evil possessors must be endured and civil law does not make them use their wealth better, but rather makes their bad use less injurious.

Paul urges the rich Christians to sell and give to the poor (Eph 5:22, 6:1-9). Was Paul influenced by Jesus? (Mt 19:27) (L 157). Is this counsel only for the perfect? No, it also applies to the weaker soul, "who remembers that he is a Christian when he hears that he must give up Christ or lose all his possessions, not placing his hope in the uncertainty of riches, but in the living God" (1 Tim 6:17).

Jesus said that if we do not renounce our earthly ties, we cannot be his disciple (Lk 14:33). How do we renounce our wealth? By not loving it and by giving to the needy; by loving Christ more and transferring our hope from our riches to Christ. Moreover, we should be ready to give them up, if our choice is between them and Christ.

What about the rich Christians who are not possessed by their

1. *On John* 6, 25.

money, but rather live in a spirit of renunciation, raising their families as good Christians, hospitable, giving food and clothes to the needy and willing to give up all for Christ, lest by losing Christ, they lose themselves along with their riches? Some wealthy Christians even gave their lives for Christ during the persecutions. Though resisting Christ's counsel to sell all, they gave up everything for Christ in their martyrdoms.

"Let them walk in the path of perfection by selling all their goods and spending the money on works of mercy. However, they should not judge others who are unable to follow the counsel, if they are truly poor in Christ." Let them rather make ready to receive into everlasting mansions — the charitable rich who have made friends of them through the mammon of iniquity (Lk 16:9). Some, who look down on mediocre Christians who hold onto their wealth, "are supported in their needs by rich and religious Christians."

The church includes soldiers and officers, vineyard and viticulturists, flock and shepherds. They are interdependent just like the wealthy laity and the servants of God.

Augustine, as we have seen, practiced the life of evangelical poverty with the help of God's grace and the support of his brethren. "He who gives up what he has and what he desires to have, gives up the whole world." Moreover, he and his friends never patronized the hardworking and charitable family man.

Augustine never criticizes the rich and tepid Christians who make good use of their wealth. But he chastises those who think themselves great because they have sold all (often not much) and yet by their condemnation of others undermine the Lord's inheritance.

Like Jesus, Augustine preaches the ideal life of a Christian, selling, giving and following Christ, the epitome of Christian monasticism through the millennia. However, this is a counsel and not a command. For Jesus still loved the rich young man who turned his back on his invitation to the life of renunciation.

Furthermore, many, if not most of the monks, were poor peasants, ex-slaves or draft dodgers.[1] So they merely moved from a life of involuntary poverty to a style of voluntary renunciation. In fact, those who gave up the least tended to live it up in the monastery. Though the monastic tradition had stressed that the monks be self-supporting, many succumbed to laziness.[2]

---

1. See J. Mohler, *The Heresy of Monasticism.*
2. See Chapter VI.

Sermons on Riches and Poverty: Interior and Exterior Riches

When yon give alms, do not be proud like the Pharisees (S 9). If you give a hundredth and others give a tenth, you still rejoice. We should not worry over others, but only over what Christ has told us to do.

In our secular desires we want to be rich. This is not so much a rising above poverty as it is a conquering of the wealthy. In the process we ignore the wall-to-wall beggars and the multitude of the poor.

Augustine says that we should not spare our transitory and vain treasures. Nor should we add up millions under the guise of family piety. What if everyone used this excuse? There would be nothing left for alms for the poor.

Why not give everything to him who made us out of nothing and nourishes us from the food he created. Is it better to give our patrimony to our sons and daughters or to our Creator? Moreover, if our sons and daughters predecease us, do we send their inheritance on to heaven? Why not give it to Christ who leads us to eternal life?

The disease of wealth is pride (1 Tim 6:17). Paul was not terrified by riches, but rather by the sickness of riches. "Great the rich man who does not consider himself great because he is rich." The other kind is at the same time proud and needy. While in the flesh he brags, in his heart he begs. Though he is inflated, he is not full.

Christ is both poor and rich. He was made poor for us that we might become enriched (2 Cor 8:9). By his death he did not earn money for us, but rather eternal life. While Christ is rich inside, outside he is poor. A rich God hidden inside a poor man. Through Christ's blood, casting off the rags of iniquity, we put on the stole of immortality.

All the good and faithful Christians are rich inside. Rich in conscience, they sleep sounder than the wealthy who lie covered with purple.

Christ never condemned the riches of the world, but rather the inane peril of riches. Among those who are affluent in faith are also those who are rich in the possessions of this world. But they should not be proud, placing their hopes in the uncertainty of luxury.

Why is the rich man proud? Because he builds his hopes on wobbly wealth. If he paid attention, he would fear. For the more money he has, the more anxiety. It is so easy to lose it all. Moreover, many of the affluent become affected and corrupt.

Most Christians ignored the advice of Jesus about not building treasures on earth. Augustine does not advise his people to get rid of their wealth, but rather to use it properly. The good Christian rich person is not inflated or lifted up by his business or financial success, but rather he stoops to help his poor brother or sister. Nor is he or she embarrassed to be seen as a brother or sister of the poor, imitating Christ who gave himself for all of his brothers and sisters.

What good are riches anyway? Do not place your hopes in incestuous goods (1 Tim 6:17-19), in a false life of purple and linen, while ignoring the beggar at the doorstep. Though the destitute one had his treasure in heaven, the affluent man was punished (Lk 16:19-26). Let the rich of the world pay attention to where their true wealth really is.

The riches of the heart: fortitude, piety, charity and faith are preferable to gold. So why seek things that please the eye? For faith shines brighter than gold. God sees this interior wealth, which we do not. Just as we have faith in our servants, so God trusts us. Since our riches come from Christ, we should confess our poverty to him, like the publican.

Though the world delights in money, honor and power, we should seek out the lower place in order to be invited up higher (Lk 14:10). Since we brought nothing with us, we should be satisfied with a humble spot (S 39).

Although money itself is good, a lust for it should be feared. For the worm of riches is pride. However, if our pride is cured, our riches will do us no harm. We should place our hopes in the money of good works. God gives the world to the rich and poor. So he who feeds the rich, feeds the poor through the rich.

When we die, we can't take our wealth along. The Lord will not let us perish if we give to him what he has given to us.

Why does God give some people riches? In order to help the poor. And he makes some people poor to test the rich (Mt 10:12). He who has more should do more. E.g. the widow's mite and Zachaeus' half. We should give alms that God will hear our prayer and bring us to eternal life.

"Mine is gold and silver," says the Lord (Hg 2:9) (S 50). The wealthy one who does not want to share money with the needy thinks that God is asking him to give up his own precious possessions rather than God's. God says, "Gold and silver are mine," not yours. Why do we hesitate to give from God's riches to help the poor? And why are we so proud when we distribute God's wealth?

Why does God give his gold to the good and the bad? If he kept it from the bad, poverty would be looked down upon as a great penance. Moreover, if gold is taken from the good, poverty would be greatly admired as the highest beatitude.

We should not call bad what is God's. The mammon of iniquity implies that there is another mammon or riches, which unless we are good, we cannot possess, that is, interior wealth (1 Pt 3:4).

Unjust riches are those which do not take away a need. For rather than bringing satiety they only inflame our lust for more. Much money does not close the gates of greed; on the other hand, it only opens them wider.

The good use of riches is a merciful treasure, that is, hospitality to the stranger, feeding the hungry, clothing the naked, etc. This the merciful good do with their gold and silver, while serving the Lord who really owns all. So gold and silver are not evil as the Manicheans say, but are misused.

We should not turn our mammon into the mammon of iniquity. Our true riches which free us from our needs should not be compared to earthly wealth, which does not take away our needs.

We praise the successful business person who sells lead and acquires gold. And yet we do not laud when riches are traded for justice. "If you want to have justice, be a beggar of God." And God the rich *pater familias* will reward us with eternal life (S 61).

We brought nothing with us, found much here and will take nothing away when we leave. It is one thing to be rich and another to desire to be rich, which leads to pride. For those who want to be rich fall into many harmful lusts. On the other hand, those who do not hope in ephemeral luxury are not proud. Furthermore, many who were rich yesterday are poor today and many who go to sleep rich wake up to find that thieves have taken everything.

We should not place all our hopes in uncertain wealth, but rather in the God who gives us all — the eternal to enjoy and the temporal to use. We should use the temporal to do good and the eternal to become good.

The rich, Augustine notes, should use their superfluous goods to help the poor, while reserving enough food and housing for their own needs. Both the rich and the poor seek to satisfy their hungers, the poor with cheap food, the rich with an expensive cuisine. But both are sated.

God made both the rich and the poor, who are companions along the same road. The poor carry nothing, while the rich are weighed down with their possessions. "Give him what you have and you feed him and, at the same time, diminish your load."

Paul notes that the poor are the rich of the other world (2 Cor 6:10) (S 85). Though a thief may steal our gold, who can take our God away? What do the rich have, if they do not have God? And what do the poor not have, if they have their God?

Some have enough, while others lack the bare necessities. Share here and you will share there. Share bread here and you will receive Bread there. What is this Bread? It is Jesus Christ (Jn 6:51). Though we may be rich here, we might be poor there. We may have a lot of gold, but not the present Christ. "Share what you have and you will receive what you do not have."

But people ask: how much should we give to the poor? Should we give up everything? Share, but do not give away everything. Keep more than a mere subsistence for yourself and your family. But we should give more than the Scribes and Pharisees, who offered one tenth (Lk 18:12).

Our true treasure should be in heaven. If our earthly wealth is stolen, our heart falls. However, if our treasure is in heaven, it rises up (S 86).

Augustine calls usury unjust for it goes against the teaching of Jesus, "I was hungry and you gave me to eat, etc." (Mt 25:31-40). The usurer wants rather to acquire wealth from the tears of the needy.

On earth we seek out our debtors to pay up. But when we give to Christ, he gives us back more. "I did not receive through me, but through mine." Moreover, what was given pertains to me. "I accepted earthly things and will give heavenly ones," the eternal Bread which is never consumed.

What does the usurer want but to give and receive money? Few give and many receive. The Lord says, "All which you gave, I will change for the better." If we give a pound of silver and receive a pound of gold, how happy we would be. Silver and gold are not similar. A fortiori, earth and heaven. Gold and silver we leave behind, while God gives us more, Eternal Life.

Avarice and luxury are contraries. For while avarice says "save!" luxury tells us to "spend!" Since neither one can order us, they persuade us through flattery. But Christ can free us from the heavy yoke of avarice and luxury.

Though God refutes the temptations of avarice, on the other hand he says the same thing, that is, save for yourself and you will have treasure in heaven.

The luxurious rich man, proud, dressed and feasted splendidly, is contrasted with the ulcerous beggar at the door seeking only crumbs (Lk 16:19-31). Yet the rich man refused to feed the poor. Jesus says: do not spare your treasures. Share what you can. Do well by your soul lest it be taken away tonight.

In a sense, everyone is poor and a beggar of God (S 123), asking him for our daily bread (Mt 6:11). Christ says, "Give me what I have given to you," for he created all that we have. "Why not give me from my own things?" Give and he will return much more. From a giver he becomes a debtor. And, in a sense, we become Christ's usurer. "You give me a little and I will give you more. You give me earthly things and I will give you heavenly ones."

Material things are by no means evil, but they can be used in an evil way. Even if we have no gold, our lust for gold remains. While some goods such as piety, faith, justice, etc., are found only in the good, others such as money, honor, power, health, etc., are common to the good and the bad.

Why does God give wealth to the bad? So that they can be countered by the good who seek the better. External goods such as gold, silver, property, clothes, patronage, servants, flocks, honors and power are earthly, temporal and transitory. If all these things were not given also to the bad, they would be considered great by the good. Therefore, God who gives goods to the evil teaches us to desire the better. Otherwise if he gives us riches, we think ourselves good and deserving.

Before the rich man had his wealth, he was humble. Then he began to be rich, contemning the poor. Why does having earthly goods make him worse? Because he is bad. But is not gold good? Yes, however evil people can do bad things with good gold, prompting us to seek the better, Christ himself.

Conclusion

As we have seen, wealthy Roman landholders exploited the poor despite emperors, Stoics and church fathers' remonstrations. Christianity began with communal living in the rabbinical *haburah* of Jesus. Yet as Christianity spread to the large multitudes including the rich and poor, this life style became less practical, though the ideal lived on in the monastic communes which strove to follow Jesus' counsel to sell all, give to the poor and follow him in voluntary poverty.

As we noted, Augustine taught the two cities, heavenly and earthly—a clue to his theology of wealth and poverty. Here below the two metropolises necessarily intermingle. But earthly goods should be used to help us attain eternal life, which alone should be enjoyed in itself. Making means such as wealth, property, power, etc., into ends in themselves is a misuse or abuse of creatures.

Augustine also teaches that we are all, rich and poor, born and die naked, the goods that we acquire during our earthly stay were all created by God. So when we share with the less fortunate we are not giving ours but God's goods.

Augustine also contrasts the real interior riches of faith, hope, love, justice, etc. with the lesser external wealth of money, honor and power.

The eternal question: why do the wicked prosper? So the good will see the way to the better. Augustine's theology of the material possessions as means to eternal life would influence later spiritualities such as the Franciscan and Jesuit.

EPILOGUE

We have seen a few of the many *quaestiones disputatae* discussed by Augustine. These are perennial puzzles which bother us today as much as they did Augustine and his friends and adversaries.

The Problem of Evil

To begin with the problem of evil which will probably never be solved to the satisfaction of all. However, Augustine opposed the Zoroastrian Manichean dualist approach which tended to see matter as evil. On the contrary, Augustine said that matter is good, for it is created by the good God. So evil is a lacuna or a privation of good. Hence evil must exist in good as a subject. Therefore, an evil person is an evil good. Consequently men and women are not essentially evil, but rather flawed by original sin and concupiscence.

At first, the evils of the world such as crime, sickness, death, earthquakes, storms, droughts, famine, war, etc. seem to militate against belief in a good God. However, we see with a narrow vision while God knows how suffering fits into the scheme of his world plan. For example, our pains can help us to correct some of our earlier mistakes.

Sins and grief are not necessary to the world. But free souls who can sin or not are necessary. Furthermore, God can bring good out of evil, which is better than not allowing any evil at all.

Faith

Augustine was a philosopher before he was a believer. And he wrestled with the conundrum of which comes first, faith or reason.

Certainly his Neoplatonism helped pave the way for his conversion. But it was the light of Christ which made the difference.

Augustine calls faith, thinking with assent. While his reason struggles to see the divine mystery, the limit of faith inspires a firm "Yes." However, our faith is not only an intellectual exercise. No, it is also affective. Thus to believe in God is to love him.

Augustine's Neoplatonic theory of knowledge he also applied to his theology of faith. Thus the divine light helps us to see the eternal truths. Moreover, without this supernatural help we cannot believe or even begin to believe.

Love

Augustine is the great Western philosopher and theologian of love. He had experienced many human loves in his life. But it was divine love which overshadowed them all, since human love is necessarily transient, while divine love is eternal.

Neoplatonism helped Augustine develop his philosophy of love, where God is *eros,* love and beauty and the object of love. He joined Neoplatonic *eros* with Christian *agape,* descent and ascent.

For Augustine our happiness consists of our possession of our chief good, namely, God. For all other loves give us a lesser joy. And since virtue is perfect love of God, all morality is based on this fundamental virtue, which includes our love of neighbor and our own self-love. Although Augustine had experienced many loves in his life, his soul is still restless until it rests in God and he loves others in him.

Evil is basically a disordered love aimed at lower goods, rather than at the highest Good. While Augustine pursues outside loves, eternal Beauty resides within. His love of God is a lightness bearing him upwards. Since God loved us first, how can we not return it?

Augustine distinguishes two types of love, *frui* and *uti,* enjoyment and use. God alone is to be enjoyed in himself, while the things of the earth are to be used to help us toward this divine union. So we should love others and ourselves in God.

Charity is when we love God for his own sake and others for God's sake, whereas lust enjoys self or neighbor without any reference to God. Moreover, charity is dear because we buy it with our very selves. Furthermore, we should spread our love of God to others and not keep it selfishly for ourselves.

Our human love models itself on the Trinity of love: Lover, Beloved and Love. Love, God, binds lover and beloved. Mind, knowledge and love; memory, understanding and love are other triads mirroring God.

The Holy Spirit, the personification of God's love, turned the early Christian church into a community of love. John's school of love balanced the Neoplatonism of Augustine's early days. Since a city is determined by its loves, the city of God is built on its love of God.

Marriage

Since Augustine had a common law wife as a student and as a young teacher, he writes from experience about love and marriage. Moreover, since he had been frequently tempted by lust he could relate to the trials of his people.

Augustine's work as a pastor taught him the need of a good theology of marriage. He followed Paul in basing the sanctity and indissolubility of matrimony on the archetypal union of Christ with his church. The good Christian wife mirrors the church, Christ's spouse. She is a woman of one husband as her partner should be a man of one wife. Like Paul, Augustine places virginity on a high plane. But the virgin should be humble and remember that virginity and marriage are mutually supportive.

Marriage is permanent because God is at its core. So Augustine opposes easy Roman divorce. He also challenges the double standard of adultery. For the husband should give good example to his wife.

Against the Manicheans Augustine writes that marriage is good, in fact, a threefold good: child, fidelity and sacrament. For Augustine as it is for Rome, Judaism and early Christianity, marriage is child-oriented, although fidelity is more important than procreation.

Augustine the Monk

The grace of God drew Augustine to the monastic way, beginning with his early philosophical discussion groups. And when he became a cleric at Hippo, he pursed the common life with his fellow clergy.

Though he had high praise for the monks and virgins of the church, Augustine did not hesitate to criticize them for vices such as pride and laziness. He is considered one of the founders of Western religious life based on charity. His rules cover everything from clothing and baths to obedience and poverty.

Augustine always saw his Christian faith along with his monastic and priestly vocations as divine gifts without any merit on his part. He has been called the patron of mediocre Christians, which means he saw ordinary men and women with all their weaknesses. Moreover, he objected to any do-it-yourself asceticism as advertised by Origen, Evagrius and Pelagius.

Christian Women

As pastor of Hippo Augustine had equal concern for the men and women of his flock. We have seen his teachings on marriage and virginity, the two great Christian vocations. Although the Judaeo-Christian tradition and Roman culture were patriarchal, yet women's liberation was growing in both. For example, Mary and the female church, the spouse of Christ, are paradigms of the good Christian woman.

Though Augustine is Roman and Pauline in naming the husband as the head of the house, nevertheless, like Jesus, he voids the old double standard of sexual mores prevalent in ancient times.

His mother Monica was Augustine's model Christian woman. Even though she suffered much from her abusive husband and her wayward son, yet she remained patient, prayerful, kind and hospitable. In her own way Monica is a leader and more influential on her son than if she had been a bishop.

Bishop Augustine was the spiritual guide to many women, teaching them from the pulpit, instructions and letters.

Augustine, Teacher

By profession Augustine had been a rhetor. And he became a Christian rhetor when he converted and ascended the episcopal chair at Hippo. He has been called the greatest pedagogue of Western Christianity, passing on his educational techniques to his clerics and catechists.

Yet he always insisted that though the words he speaks or writes are his, it is Christ who is the interior instructor of all. As Paul taught — there is only one Master.

Social Justice

Most cultures look back on a golden age when all were equal and shared in God's bounty. Jews, Christians and Romans alike enjoyed these dreams. Though this halcyon common life was not practical in the property-conscious Roman empire, nevertheless, many Christians, including Augustine, practiced some sort of communism based, at least in part, on the counsel of Jesus to the rich young man.

The Stoics, Jews and Christian Fathers stressed a sharing of the world's goods with the less fortunate, and this is to be done in justice, not in charity. After all, God owns everything anyway and we are just his stewards. So we really do not own anything absolutely.

Like the Stoics, Augustine valued the interior wealth of the virtues over external riches. Following his earlier distinction of *frui* and *uti,* enjoyment and use, he said that our material possessions are not to be enjoyed in themselves, but rather are to be used to help us on the road to our final Good.

Finis

We have seen Augustine's views on a few major subjects. He has much to say to us today. However, we should read him against his fifth century Christian Roman background. But what makes him a classical author is his ability to narrate his personal beliefs in a way that mirrors those of many of us through the ages. For example, the problem of evil, a doubting faith, youthful loves and marriage, religious vocation, his studies and teaching and finally his balanced view of this world's wealth, successes and happiness.

ABBREVIATIONS

A   *Ancient Christian Writers,* J. Quasten et al., eds., New York, Paulist/Newman

F   *Fathers of the Church,* R. Deferrari, ed., Washington, Catholic University Press

L   Letters

LC Loeb Classical Library, Cambridge, Harvard University Press

N   *A Select Library of the Nicene and Post-Nicene Fathers,* Second Series, P. Schaff and H. Wade, eds., Grand Rapids, Eerdmans

P   *Patrologiae Cursus Completus,* J.-P. Migne, ed., Paris

S   Sermons

SC *Sources Chrétiennes,* H. DeLubac and J. Daniélou, eds., Paris, Cerf

A SELECTED BIBLIOGRAPHY

Augustine's Works

The Works of Saint Augustine—A Translation for the 21st Century, New York, New City Press, 1989-.

Patrologia Latina, Paris, Migne, 1844-64.

Corpus Christianorum Ecclesiasticorum Latinorum, Vienna, 1866-.

Corpus Christianorum, Series Latina, Turnai, Brepols, 1955-.

Oeuvres, Bibliothéque Augustinnienne, Paris, Desclée de Brouwer, 1949-.

Biblioteca de Autores Cristianos, Madrid, La Editorial Católica, 1944-.

Sources Chrétiennes, Paris, Cerf, 1960-.

Ancient Christian Writers, Westminster, Newman, 1944-.

A Select Library of the Nicene and Post-Nicene Fathers of the Christian Church, Buffalo, Schaff, 1886-1888.

Fathers of the Church, Washington, Catholic University Press, 1960-.

Some Books on Augustine

Bardy, G., *Saint Augustin,* Paris, Desclée de Brouwer, 1948.

Batterhouse, R., et al., *A Companion to the Study of St. Augustine,* Oxford U. Press, 1955.

Bourke, V., *Augustine's Quest of Wisdom,* Milwaukee, Bruce, 1945.

———., *The Essential Augustine,* New York, Mentor-Omega, 1964.

Brown, P., *Augustine of Hippo,* Berkeley, University of California Press, 1967.

———., *Religion and Society in the Age of Saint Augustine,* New York, Harper and Row, 1972.

Chadwick, H., *Augustine,* New York, Oxford University Press, 1986.

D'Arcy, M., et al., *St. Augustine,* Cleveland, World, 1960.

Fortman, E., *The Triune God,* A Historical Study of the Trinity, Grand Rapids, Baker, 1982.

Gilson, E., *The Christian Philosophy of St. Augustine,* New York, Random House, 1960.

Grabowski, S., *The All Present God, A Study of St. Augustine*, St. Louis, Herder, 1953.

————., *The Church, An Introduction to the Study of St. Augustine*, St. Louis, Herder, 1957.

Hawkins, A. H., *Archetypes of Conversion: Autobiographies of Augustine*, Bunyan and Merton, Lewisburg, Bucknell University Press, 1985.

Markus, R. A., *Saeculum, History and Society in the Theology of Saint Augustine*, Cambridge University Press, 1970.

Marrou, H., *St. Augustine and His Influence Through the Ages*, New York, Harper and Row, 1957.

Marshall, M., *The Restless Heart, The Life and Influence of St. Augustine*, Grand Rapids, Eerdmans, 1987.

Meer, F. van der, *Augustine, the Bishop, The Life and Work of a Father of the Church*, New York, Sheed and Ward, 1961.

Mourant, H., *An Introduction to the Philosophy of St. Augustine, Selected Readings and Commentaries*, University Park, Pennsylvania University Press, 1964.

Nash, R., *The Light of the Mind, St. Augustine's Theory of Knowledge*, Lexington, University Press of Kentucky, 1969.

Oates, W., *Basic Writings of St. Augustine*, New York, Random House, 1964.

O'Daly, G. J., *Augustine's Philosophy of Mind*, Berkeley, University of California Press, 1987.

O'Donnell, J. J., *Augustine*, Boston, Twayne, 1985.

O'Meara, J., *The Young Augustine: The Growth of St. Augustine's Mind up to His Conversion*, Toronto, Longmans, 1954.

O'Toole, C., *The Philosophy of Creation in the Writings of St. Augustine*, Washington, Catholic University Press, 1944.

Pelikan, J., *The Mystery of Continuity: Time and History, Memory and Eternity in the Thought of St. Augustine*, Charlottesville, University Press of Virginia, 1986.

Pellegrino, M., *The True Priest: The Priesthood as Preached and Practiced by St. Augustine*, Villanova, Augustinian Press, 1988.

Pope, H., *The Teaching of St. Augustine on Prayer and the Contemplative Life*, London, Burns, Oates and Washbourne, 1935.

————., *St. Augustine of Hippo*, Garden City, Doubleday, 1961.

Portaglié, E., *A Guide to the Thought of St. Augustine*, Chicago, Regnery, 1960.

Pryzwara, E., *An Augustine Synthesis*, New York, Harper and Row, 1958.

Rotelle, J., ed., *Augustine Day by Day*, Villanova, Augustinian Press.

Te Selle, E., *Augustine, the Theologian*, New York, Herder and Herder, 1970.

Trapé, A., ed., *My Mother, by Saint Augustine of Hippo*, Villanova, Augustinian Press.

Ulanov, B., *Prayers of Saint Augustine*, Villanova, Augustinian Press.

Wolfson, H., *The Philosophy of the Church Fathers*, Cambridge, Harvard University Press, 1956.

Zumkeller, A., *Augustine's Rule*, Villanova, Augustinian Press.

————., *Augustine's Ideal of the Religious Life*, Villanova, Augustinian Press.

INDEX